PRAISE FOR FROM BULLY TO BULL'S-EYE

"Emotions matter, and matter a great deal at work. They guide complex decision making, help people build and maintain positive relationships, and influence psychological wellbeing. *From Bully to Bull's-Eye* provides a clear pathway for employees and managers to create psychologically healthy, emotionally intelligent workplaces so that all stakeholders can thrive personally and professionally."

—MARC A. BRACKETT, PH.D. Director, Yale Center for
Emotional Intelligence

"I worked with Andrew Faas for a number of years and what he advocates in *From Bully to Bull's-Eye* is something he has effectively put into practice, particularly in building positive, high performance cultures."

—GLENN MURPHY, Former Chairman and Chief Executive
Officer of Gap Inc.

"Faas transforms workplace bullying from a non-issue that many managers dismiss as unimportant into a full-blown psychological and business emergency. This issue can't be dealt with anywhere but at the very top of successful organizations. *From Bully to Bull's-Eye* will wake many businesspeople up to the realities of the modern workplace, and hopefully help them change their environments into ones of psychological and emotional safety."

—PAUL GIONFRIDDO, President and CEO of Mental Health
America

From Bully to Bull's-Eye

From Bully to Bull's-Eye

Move Your Organization
Out of the Line of Fire

Andrew Faas

Far too many employees around the world live in fear.

To them I dedicate this book.

TABLE OF CONTENTS

Part Four: Guidance and Advice

Is Your Workplace Psychologically Safe?

"The workplace is the most dangerous place to be
in America."
–US DEPARTMENT OF JUSTICE (GRIMME)

Abuse // Coercion // Discrediting // Exploitation //
Extortion // Harassment // Intimidation //
Threats = Bullying in the Workplace

Is your workplace psychologically safe? This is the question that everyone in an organization, at every level, should be asking in a critical way.

Many people I have spoken to, when they hear the word "bullying," relate it to what occurs in schools and usually think what goes on in the workplace is the norm. They do not associate the actions or behaviors with bullying. However, when I describe the dynamics of bullying, which include the words "abuse," "coercion," "exploitation," "extortion," "harassment" and "threats," it instantly resonates and people acknowledge the unnecessary stress caused by bullying.

During and after writing my first book, *The Bully's Trap: Bullying in the Workplace*, I received a lot of pushback from executives who believe that my findings and assertions are extreme exaggerations. Most claim the level of discontent and fear is not the case in their organizations, citing positive engagement surveys, robust policies and procedures, methods by which employees can provide honest feedback, enlightened human resource professionals, and sensitivity, diversity and sexual harassment training.

My usual response is that they are fortunate and unique, because this is not the case in most organizations. Most mid-sized to large organizations have all of the elements in place that defensive executives cite, yet most of these organizations are not truly psychologically healthy, safe and fair. The research I completed and comments I received since the book was published suggest that my earlier findings and assertions were definitely not extreme exaggerations. In fact, the findings do not adequately describe how bad it is out there.

My initial mission in writing *The Bully's Trap* was to start a debate about that very subject. However, over the course of my journey learning about workplace bullying, I discovered that the issue is much broader than that. It's not just a matter of bullying in the workplace—entire workplace cultures in many organizations are built on foundational principles that guarantee a toxic environment for all, not just a few select victims of particularly vitriolic harassment.

Gallup polling shows that more than 70 percent of North American workers are not engaged. My findings suggest that most are not engaged because they do not respect and/or trust their bosses and, by extension, the organization itself; and many spend the bulk of their waking hours living in fear. Case in point: a Harvard study called "The Relationship between Workplace Stressors and Mortality and Health Costs in the United States" reports that more than 120,000 deaths annually may be attributable to workplace stress.

Since the publication of *The Bully's Trap*, there have been numerous examples of psychologically unsafe workplaces in the press, the most notable being Amazon, Wells Fargo and Volkswagen, which I will get into in more detail in the book. These examples reinforce some of the findings and assertions I made in *The Bully's Trap*. Unfortunately, in politics, Donald Trump has become a role model for what I refer to as the CBO, or Chief Bullying Officer.

It is a basic and fundamental right of everyone to live, learn, worship, work and play in a safe and protected environment.

An unsafe environment is one in which people are physically and mentally harmed, and/or under the threat of being harmed. Bullying is the most common dynamic in a psychologically unsafe environment. The issue of school bullying has received considerable exposure, largely due to the incidences of suicide where bullying is a factor. By comparison, there is relatively little published material on workplace bullying that raises awareness about it, discusses its effects on employees, and provides practical prevention solutions—the prerequisite being: creating a psychologically safe and productive workplaces.

Considering how little substantive research has been conducted on the field of workplace bullying, I have been working together with my foundation, The Faas Foundation, and the Yale Center for Emotional Intelligence to launch an extensive survey that will gather evidence about the organizational benefits of psychologically safe workplaces. The goal of the survey, called the Emotion Revolution in the Workplace, is to understand how employees feel about work, and why they feel the way they do. Additionally, the Emotion Revolution will analyze how these emotions impact key outcomes, like employee physical and mental wellness, individual and organizational performance, and other important workplace elements like creativity, innovation and freedom of expression. The survey will be comprehensive in that it will gather opinions from all levels of employment and from a widespread collection of different job markets. The study is patterned after a similar initiative conducted by Yale on high school students across the U.S.

While there are some overt similarities between school and workplace bullying, workplace bullying is far more subtle and complex. Most targeted individuals do not realize what is happening to them until they are well into the situation (usually too late) and become what the bully wants them to become: a poor performer with a bad attitude—the villain rather than the victim.

You will note that I have not devoted much of this work to the rehabilitation of the bullies. Many believe bullying is a learned behavior and can be unlearned. This may or may not be true; however, I question the efficacy of this. Rather, the focus here is, as Oscar Wilde so aptly put it, "It's the prisons, not the prisoners who need the reformation." Bullies bully because they can. In many organizations, they are considered the heroes, and people at the top condone, accept and even expect bullying and fear as a motivational method. It is also interesting to note more than 70 percent of bullying is by the boss to the employee.

Psychologically unsafe workplaces have catastrophic consequences. They can ruin careers, destroy family units, ruin organizations, cause people to attempt or commit suicide, and kill others.

Creating a psychologically safe and productive workplace is everyone's responsibility; however, it must be driven and led by the very top—the Board of Directors and the CEO.

In *From Bully to Bull's-Eye*, I challenge those who work in toxic cultures to become witnesses, defenders, and activists, never having to regret saying:

- I could have prevented the ruining of my coworker's career.

- I could have prevented the break-up of a family unit.

- I could have helped prevent the demise of an organization.

- I could have deterred a suicide or attempted suicide.

- I could have prevented someone from killing others.

Everyone Has a Story

As of this writing, I have had discussions or interviews about psychologically safe workplaces with more than 600 individuals over a five-year period. Almost everyone I spoke with had a story about their own experiences or that of someone close to them.

Throughout the book, I relate some of the stories I heard. These stories will put into context what I describe in the book, particularly organizational cultural dynamics, the ways and means of abuse, and the devastating effects that a psychologically unsafe environment can have.

The people I have discussed this with, or interviewed, are from Canada, the United States, Israel and Europe. They represent a cross-section of sectors, private, public and not-for-profit, governments, manufacturing, retail, healthcare, resources, transportation and financial services.

All of the discussions and interviews were unstructured. I just let people talk, relaying their experiences and those of their family members, friends or coworkers. Rarely did I have to interject to seek clarification. For almost everyone, the experience is still fresh in their minds, because they keep reliving it. One common issue is an inability to find closure. For those who read *The Bully's Trap* and those I had discussions and interviews with, being able to talk about it brought some degree of closure.

In listening to their stories, I tried to categorize the experiences of people who work in a psychologically unsafe workplace in the following categories:

- Reason for being targeted

- Ways and means of bullying

- Reporting or exposing

- Organizational response

- Coping and/or reacting

- Impact on physical and mental health, family, friends and employment

- Roles bystanders played

- Post bullying outcomes

I do not claim this is a scientific study; however, what I heard was consistent with research on the topic. The following outlines what was expressed:

- In more than 70 percent of the cases, the bullying was done by boss to worker.

- The main reason people were targeted was to get rid of them.

- Most of the targets got caught in the bully's trap: becoming the villain rather than the victim.

- Most of the cases involved psychological bullying.

- In most cases, intimidation and threats were made, usually related to being let go or demoted.

- Just under half of employees left the organization because of bullying.

- Those who left had difficulty getting re-established.

- More than one-third experienced some form of sexual harassment.

- Almost all tried to deal with the situation alone, tending to make excuses for the bullying or blaming themselves and/or denying or minimizing abuse as a way to survive it.

- Most, to varying degrees, developed physical health problems.

- Just under 70 percent reported symptoms consistent with Post Traumatic Stress Disorder (PTSD).

- Almost everyone indicated that the experience had a negative effect on their relationship with family members and close friends. Many became bullies at home.

- Just over one-third considered suicide.

- Almost two-thirds described the CEO of their organization as a bully.

- A culture of fear existed in most of the organizations.

- More than 60 percent were forced to engage in and/or observe unethical and or illegal activities.

- Most would not report wrongdoing.

- Most do not trust the feedback mechanisms in place (engagement surveys, 360 feedback, employee assistance programs or whistleblower hot lines).

- In fewer than 10 percent of the cases bystanders become witnesses, defenders or resistors.

- Where the bystanders did become witnesses, defenders or resistors, most were retaliated against.

- Bystanders became complicit in more than half of the cases.

- In the few cases where there was an investigation, there was an unsatisfactory outcome.

- Close to three-quarters of the organizations had workplace violence/bullying/harassment policies and procedures in place. Most felt they were meaningless.

- More than 80 percent felt that the Human Resource department in their organizations was part of the problem.

- Everyone who was unionized complained that the union failed to properly represent their interests.

- Almost everyone had difficulty in finding closure, even long after the bullying stopped.

My story

As indicated, I offer unique perspectives on the topic, through the lens of a bully, bystander, witness, defender, resistor, activist and target. Here is my story:

Early in my career, I had the benefit of having a coach who influenced my management and leadership philosophy for life.

Bob McCutcheon, a senior executive at Loblaw Companies Limited (Canada's largest food retailer), appeared in my office early one morning, sat down, and took out his pipe (they allowed smoking in those days).

As he prepared his pipe (a long, drawn-out process), he started.

"Son, I have a major problem. You see, there is a young manager; he is cocky, overly aggressive to the point of being abrasive, not sensitive to others, unreasonably demanding, doesn't listen to others, and bullies people to get things done. I'm totally perplexed on what to do."

Flattered that Bob, who was considered the senior statesman, would come to me with such a weighty issue, I quickly said, "I would fire the SOB."

After taking a long drag from his pipe, Bob responding by saying, "Well, son, that's my dilemma. You're the SOB I am talking about."

Thankfully, Bob did not follow my advice but, for me, it was a lifelong coaching lesson and I went on to become, at age 29, the youngest vice president in the organization and enjoyed a 23-year career with them.

After this intervention, and throughout my career, I focused on becoming a better manager and leader through mutual respect, which has made me and the organizations I led successful beyond my wildest dreams.

The first step was to gain a deep understanding about:

- How employees feel about their work,

- Why employees feel the way they do,

- The extent to which employees feel they are working to their full potential, and

- The barriers to being able to work to full potential.

In addition, find out from people who were in a supervisory role:

- How they think their employees feel, and

- How they want their employees to feel.

Having the benefit of this information, I was able to create psychologically safe workplaces that significantly reduced or eliminated the unnecessary stress factors and barriers to people working to their full potential. A key component of this was the creation of a value-exchange model, based on the ethic of reciprocity (which I will describe more fully in the section on performance management).

Also, throughout my career, I have been involved with numerous bullying situations, not only helping employees cope with, and resolve, what they were going through, but more importantly, get at the root cause which, in most instances, resulted in a shift in culture and attitude.

Late in my career, I became a target in retaliation for blowing the whistle on a corrupt executive. The Board of Directors asked whether they could use my name as the source of the accusations, which, because I trusted them, I agreed to. The executive intimidated the board to the point that I became the villain rather than the victim.

For an 18-month period, I went through sheer hell. In attempts to discredit me, my phones were tapped, my emails were hacked, and a private investigator, on the company's dime, was hired to follow me. During this period, I received a death threat, my associates shunned me, and I was blacklisted in the Canadian business community.

This was the worst experience I ever had; I lost more than 30 pounds; was laid up for six months with a serious case of shingles, and had symptoms consistent with Post Traumatic Stress

Disorder (PTSD). I became withdrawn, irritable and my relationships with friends and family were severely tested.

Thankfully, the truth was ascertained, the executive was forced out, and I was able to negotiate a settlement with the organization.

This, however, did not end the situation for me because I could not find closure. During those 18 months it consumed most of my waking hours and, I must admit, it haunts me to this day.

About three months after the situation was resolved, while still wallowing in self pity, I realized how fortunate I was having the situation end to my satisfaction because I had the background, experience and resources to deal with it, which most who are targeted do not. This caused me to reflect on how I could shift all of this negative energy into something positive. The answer was obvious in that I was in a unique position to help those who are going through the horrors of being bullied and perhaps, more importantly, influence significant change in the way organizations operate by creating psychologically safe and productive cultures.

The Bully's Trap was the starting point in opening a debate and discussion about the topic. From this, my foundation, the Faas Foundation, has partnered with two world-class organizations: Mental Health America and the Yale Center for Emotional Intelligence on major initiatives to help organizations create psychologically safe and productive cultures.

From victim to villain: Vera's story

In July of 2010, Vera was given the option to resign or be fired from her position as a marketing manager for an appliance manufacturer, a position she held for nine years. The reasons given for her termination were poor performance and insubordination. Not wanting to jeopardize her ability to relocate, she agreed to resign and received a modest severance.

Vera's last formal performance review was in February of 2009, when she received an "exceeds expectations" rating. She also received an above average merit increase and an incentive payout recognizing that she met all of her individual performance objectives. Over the previous eight years, Vera was rated and viewed as a high performer.

In August of 2009, as part of a restructuring, Vera's reporting relationship changed, and Mark, who was also a marketing manager, became the director of the department and Vera's boss. Vera felt that she was more qualified than Mark, but recognized that he had more of a presence, which, in the culture of the organization, counted for more. While Vera was disappointed that she was not promoted, she indicated to Mark that she would support him.

When they were peers, Mark viewed Vera as a threat. He would upstage her when the opportunity presented itself, and he was credited for work she did. Vera's former boss recognized this, and would tell her not to worry about it, that this was part of Mark's aggressive nature; she would get credit for her contributions. Over the years, Vera and Mark were equally exposed to senior executives to review marketing plans and major initiatives. Usually, Vera did most of the prep work and Mark made the presentation. Vera was okay with this as she was not comfortable with public speaking. During the discussion periods, however, it was apparent that Vera was better prepared than Mark, manifesting a classic case of style over substance.

When Mark became the director, he started excluding Vera from the monthly marketing review meetings with senior management. Vera continued to prepare the presentations and her only feedback came when Mark could not answer a question, blaming Vera for not having prepped him well enough. For subsequent meetings, Vera added yet more notes for Mark to reference, anticipating the questions he would be asked. Mark continued to struggle during the discussion periods. When the CEO suggested publicly that Vera should attend the meetings, Mark was concerned about Vera showing him up, and jeopardizing his position. Mark resolved to get rid of Vera.

Mark met with his boss and Tim, the head of Human Resources, to voice his dissatisfaction with Vera's work, and to let her go. They challenged Mark based on Vera's favorable performance reviews and the previous director's high opinion of her. Mark countered that the previous director covered up Vera's deficiencies, that he (Mark) carried most of the weight, and Vera resented his promotion. He also insinuated that Vera and the previous director had more than a professional relationship. The head of Human Resources told Mark that to fire Vera he had to build a case.

So he did. He kept important information from her, excluded her from meetings, gave her unrealistic targets and timelines and constantly badgered her. This affected her performance and her attitude. When she challenged Mark, he reprimanded her citing insubordination, sending copies to the vice president and Tim. Each time a mistake was made, a target or timeline not reached, Vera received a written warning, again, with copies to the vice president and Tim. In addition to the written warnings, Vera was subjected to verbal abuse, threats, and intimidation.

Knowing Mark as she did, it occurred to Vera that she was being set up. Because Mark could prove that her performance was deteriorating, she started to blame herself for the position she was in. This made her increasingly irritable, causing more confrontations with Mark, giving Mark even more ammunition.

Others in the department observed some of what was going on and most had their own challenges with Mark. Vera previously had a good working relationship with them; most sought her help, which she readily gave. When it became apparent that she was targeted, the department shunned her and she became the subject of a lot of water cooler chats. Mark fed the gossip mill by telling people how poorly Vera was handling the situation and that she "did not have her boyfriend there to protect her."

Because of her frustration with the situation and herself, she started lashing out at others in the department. This strained relationships and was a factor in no one coming to her defense. They rationalized that Vera was not handling the situation well. Mark sent some of them to Tim to complain about Vera. Some only went because they were afraid not to, while others happily complied.

Vera's doctor strongly recommended that she go on disability for stress. But Tim told her that the company wouldn't pay disability benefits, as they didn't consider stress a disability. He further told her that it would be viewed as avoiding disciplinary action for her performance and attitude, and her absence would be without cause, which would result in termination. Vera decided not to go on disability.

Not knowing what to do next, Vera complained to Tim that Mark was bullying her and setting her up to be fired. Tim defended Mark's actions and behaviors, suggesting that the issue was Vera's performance and attitude and, unless there was significant improvement, the company would have no choice but to terminate her. Tim suggested that they meet with Mark to discuss it. Vera was not comfortable with this, but felt she had no choice.

At the meeting, Tim told Mark that Vera had lodged a complaint about being bullied. Mark told Vera and Tim that he was not bullying, but only doing his job, correcting deficiencies and reacting when he felt that Vera was not being respectful. He went on to say that he was sorry that Vera felt the way she did, that he meant no harm. Tim suggested that this was more of a personality clash and Mark's style may be a bit aggressive. Mark agreed with this assessment and promised to work on his communication with Vera, adding, "I understand you are still upset with not getting the promotion, but for this to work you have to get over it."

After the meeting, Mark followed Vera into her office, closed the door and said, "Now you really have gone too f—ing far! How dare you accuse me of bullying? You're the one who started all of this, you have never been any good and you never will be. Why don't you do everyone a favor and quit?" Vera burst into tears and slapped Mark across the face.

Mark picked up the phone, called Tim, and said, "I want you to fire that bitch right now. She just hit me."

Without getting Vera's side of the story, Tim gave Vera the option to be fired or resign.

The bullying did not stop there.

An advertising agency with whom the company had a long-standing relationship thought highly of Vera and offered to hire her with the understanding that she would not be assigned any work related to her previous employer. When Mark learned of their intent, he told the agency CEO, "If you hire her, you will lose this account." Vera was not hired and is still looking for employment. She has been blacklisted and, because it's a small world, it is almost impossible for her to gain comparable employment in her field.

Part One:

Is Your Workplace Culture

a Ticking Time Bomb?

"It is not the prisoners who need reformation,
it is the prisons."
—OSCAR WILDE 1897

The Definition of a Bully

T r u m p. (Perhaps the shortest chapter on record—but need I say more?)

What's Culture Got to Do with It?

"... ordinary people, simply doing their jobs, and without any particular hostility on their part, can become agents in a terrible destructive process. Moreover, even when the destructive effects of their work become patently clear, and they are asked to carry out actions incompatible with fundamental standards of morality, relatively few people have the resources needed to resist authority"
–STANLEY MILGRAM "OBEDIENCE TO AUTHORITY"

Bullies bully because they work in environments that allow, condone, encourage, and even expect it. For the bullying to stop, a cultural transformation is required where bullying is not allowed—period!

Rarely a day goes by when there is not a story in the media about abuse of power, inappropriate behavior, corruption and greed on the part of leadership in every segment of our society, worldwide. Whether it is business, industry, government, education, social services, military, police, sports, media, entertainment, not-for-profit, or religion, not one is immune.

Where this occurs in organizations, in most cases, there also exists a culture of fear.

Reviewing recent examples of organizations that have gone down, or lost reputational value, the wrongdoing that led to the downfall could have been avoided if people within the organization who were "in the know" came forward and exposed the situation.

I assert that the last financial meltdown could have been avoided if there were not a culture of fear in those organizations that created the last financial meltdown.

AIG, Bear Stearns and Lehman Brothers are good examples of cultures of fear. Additionally, all three had CEOs who were also CBOs (Chief Bullying Officers). Ultimately, all three CEOs lost their jobs as they led their organizations over the precipice.

The Rise and Fall of Bear Stearns by Alan Greenberg is great reading for anyone in a leadership role. The book effectively describes how an organization went from having what I describe as a Stable culture to a Dictatorial culture, and the consequences of this shift. He also acknowledges that, as Chairman of the Board, he had little patience for people complaining about the CEO, mistakenly believing that they were personality or style issues.

Alan Greenberg also notes in the book that, had he paid closer attention to the indicators of the cultural shift, he would have been able to write a book titled, *The Rise and Continued Rise of Bear Stearns*.

NEVER UNDERESTIMATE HOW DEEPLY EMBEDDED THE CULTURE IS

The Volkswagen scandal is representative of the issues confronting whistle-blowers— and everyone around them—on many levels. Disclosure that the company systemically reported false fuel economy and carbon dioxide

readings points to a corporate-wide environment of fear: fear of honest communications
with management; fear of meeting performance
standards (or not); and fear of repercussions
amongst managers and colleagues.

On the heels of the scandal, and attempts
to discover the culprits and the extent of the
problem, VW suspended numerous employees
during the investigation. They know that many
are innocent, but have done so with the stated
intent that their jobs will be restored once they
have clarity. Employees who stepped forward
with information prior to the end of November
2015 were offered corporate amnesty, but still
faced civil prosecution. Employees found to
know anything who did not step forward were
warned they would be prosecuted to the full
extent of the law and corporate abilities.

The consequences of being any part of this
corporation and its culture of fear and blame
are vast and pervasive—and led to even more
fear: fear of prosecution, job loss, reputation,
income and security—even after management changed at the top. The simple fact that
employees were afraid to admit they hadn't
achieved their impossible goals has turned the
legal, personal and professional lives of everyone who was there upside down. The ensuing
investigation is creating even more of the same.

As recently as March 2016, a fired American
VW employee claims that the company
has continued destroying data despite a
Department of Justice injunction against doing
so. He is suing the company for wrongful termination citing the "whistleblower law," claiming
that he was terminated because he attempted
to stop the data deletions. The U.S. CEO
resigned two days later, agreeing that the company "totally screwed up."

GM's CEO and chairwoman, Mary Barra, provides an alternative approach to scandal compared with VW's disgrace. Confronted with a grave safety crisis that cost 124 lives, 2.6 million recalled vehicles, and over $900 billion, Barra apologized to the public, owned up to faults and rectified the cultural issues within GM that allowed the safety issues to go ignored. In contrast, VW has done everything it can to sweep details and news of their wrongdoing under the proverbial rug.

EMPLOYEES CAN BANK ON GETTING THE BLAME

In Los Angeles, some Wells Fargo employees have been fired for gaming, but others have been promoted or otherwise rewarded, alleges a lawsuit the city filed against the bank.

Driven by overwhelming sales pressure, Wells Fargo Bank employees issued unwanted credit cards and opened unauthorized accounts that charged customers fees and damaged their credit.

The lawsuit focuses mostly on what's known in the industry as bundling, also called cross-selling, where bank employees try to sell multiple bank products to a customer who may have just come in to open an account or apply for a credit card. Customers with Mexican identification cards were particularly targeted because they don't have Social Security numbers, making opening accounts easier, according to the suit.

The lawsuit says Wells Fargo executives pushed branch employees to sell a certain number of financial products each day, even if there wasn't the foot traffic available to meet those quotas. Employees were also encouraged to sell multiple products to family members and friends to meet quotas.

While Wells Fargo blames the problems on rogue employees who have been disciplined or fired, "The result is that Wells Fargo has generated a virtual fee-generating machine, through which its customers are harmed, its employees take the blame, and Wells Fargo reaps the profit," the lawsuit claims.

While the obvious victims here are the customers whose credit was compromised, the employees who worked under so much pressure that they felt compelled to cheat friends and family, in addition to strangers, were also victimized. In addition to the presumed family troubles this causes, many will take the fall for the corporation, making them twice-over victims.

People do not come forward because they fear retaliation. Consider what Sherron Watkins, the Enron whistleblower, went through after she exposed the wrongdoing there. After sending a detailed letter to the CEO detailing her concerns about Enron's accounting procedures, her job was threatened, she was eventually forced to testify to Congress and she was both lauded and vilified for her whistleblowing role in the scandal.

Many organizations have put policies, procedures and whistleblower hot lines in place to provide a mechanism for people to file reports. The sad reality is that most people do not trust it, largely because they do not trust their leaders.

In December of 2010, Sheila Fraser, who was the Auditor General of Canada, issued a scathing 375-page report on the tenure of Canada's first Public Sector Integrity Commissioner Christiane Ouimet. This department is responsible for investigating complaints of government wrongdoing by public service employees. From August 2007 to July 2009, 228 reports were filed. Of these, only seven (yes, seven!) were investigated; five were closed with no finding of wrongdoing, and two remained under investigation!

Also in her investigation, the Auditor General found that Ms. Ouimet bullied her staff; she "yelled, swore, marginalized and intimidated" certain PSIC employees and engaged in reprisals. Turnover of staff during Ms. Ouimet's tenure was an astounding 50 percent for each of her two years in office.

On July 18, 2011, Nick Davies of *The Guardian* tells how Sean Hoare (now deceased) broke the story that destroyed Rupert Murdoch's *News of the World*, humiliating the media mogul. In explaining why he came forward, he said, "I want to right a wrong, lift the lid on it, the whole culture. I know—we all know—that the hacking and other stuff is endemic. Because there is so much intimidation in the newsroom, you have people being fired, breaking down in tears, hitting the bottle."

> "Crime is a logical extension of the sort of behavior that is often considered perfectly respectable in legitimate business."
> —ROBERT RICE (FORMER ATTORNEY GENERAL), *THE BUSINESS OF CRIME*

My own research identified the following problems that are evident in unsafe cultures. Specifically:

- Leaders score low on the respectability scale.

- There is a disproportionate focus on the short-term results at the expense of sustainable long-term performance.

- Leaders do not appreciate the risks to brand and reputational value when bullying is exposed.

- Leaders condone lax ethical standards.

- People are considered expendable.

- There is subjectivity and ambiguity in performance management and advancement.

- Fear is a substitute for motivation.

- There are few checks and balances.

- There is little transparency and few disclosures.

- There is negligence at the governance level.

- Turf and power are jealously guarded.

- Power can become addictive. Those who abuse power feed on the fear they create.

The worst mining disaster in the U.S. in more than 40 years was a rare case where a guilty CEO paid a price—however slight—for his bullying and flagrant flaunting of the law. However, the verdict and sentencing were a relative tap on the wrist in exchange for the loss of 29 lives on top of certain health issues for the miners.

In 2010, in the middle of the workday, a massive explosion blew out miles of populated underground tunnels at the Upper Big Branch Mine owned by Massey Energy, which was headed up by CEO Don Blankenship.

Despite the revelation of multiple infractions of legislated mine safety and a history of bullying and harassment, because of lack of evidence, Mr. Blankenship was only convicted of conspiracy to willfully violate mine safety laws—a misdemeanor.

Sentenced in April of 2016, he received the harshest possible sentence in slight compensation for the light conviction: he received a year in federal prison and a $250,000 fine.

One of the miners, Tommy Davis, who lost his son, nephew and brother in the disaster, characterized the verdict and sentencing this way: "He's standing up there and he's hugging them people. I don't hug nothing but a damn tombstone. I hold a picture. I don't get no grandchildren."

What Is Culture?

Culture is all about hardcore business issues. Culture is all encompassing. It is how an organization:

- is governed
- is led
- is aligned to values, beliefs, principles, purpose, vision and initiatives
- is structured
- communicates
- makes decisions
- assigns and aligns work
- operates
- measures performance
- holds accountability
- rewards and recognizes
- hires people
- develops people
- advances people

- handles risk

- handles crisis

- gets information

- reacts to information

- understands how stakeholders feel

Diana Baumrind, a clinical and developmental psychologist in the 1960s, identified the three parenting styles that influence family culture as: Authoritarian, Permissive, and Authoritative.

Similarly, organizational cultures can be categorized into three distinct types:

The Dictatorial

The Disjointed

and

The Stable

I encourage you to examine your workplace under these conceptual lenses. In doing this, it is important to note that these models are not categorical; they are more of a continuum to gain an understanding. You will find that your organization or department best fits one type; however, the dominant ethos within your workplace culture will be the strongest indicator where your workplace fits on the continuum.

The Dictatorial Culture

"Dictatorship, by whatever name, is founded on the
doctrine that the individual amounts to nothing;
that the State is the only thing that counts; and
that men and women and children were put on
earth solely for the purpose of serving the State."
–HARRY S. TRUMAN

Dictatorial culture, whether in a country or an organization, is all about strictly enforcing control over its citizens or employees. Bullies thrive in a dictatorship and are considered heroes.

In this environment, people (including the bullies) live and work in fear. I have interviewed some who describe their leaders as benevolent dictators in that they portray themselves as demanding, but have the best interests of their employees in mind.

Alaa al Aswany, in *On the State of Egypt: A Novelist's Provocative Reflections*, wrote, "The concept of the benevolent dictator, just like the concepts of the noble thief or the honest whore, is no more than a meaningless fantasy." A dictator uses whatever means to achieve what s/he wants, including charm and benevolence. The true character comes out when s/he is crossed or does not achieve what s/he wants. On the effectiveness of a Dictatorial culture, Emilia Pardo Bazan put it so well when she wrote, "The dictatorship is like an aria that never becomes an opera."

The characteristics of a Dictatorial culture:

- The boss is a tyrant.

- Managers blindly follow the boss's lead.

- Bullying is a means of survival (and advancement).

- Blind obedience is expected.

- It is hierarchical and bureaucratic.

- The boss is not told what needs to be heard.

- People who "suck up" are favored.

- When things go wrong, employees are blamed and punished.

- Innovation, loyalty, good husbandry and good will are nonexistent.

- There is little to no transparency.

- There is an obsession with secrecy.

- Blind obedience is expected.

- Turf is jealously guarded.

Leon Festinger in *A Theory of Cognitive Dissonance* asserts that cultures can alter human behavior. Festinger argues that people will change their "attitudes, beliefs and actions" and/or rationalize the changes by "justifying, blaming and denying." Further, he notes that "People can be highly impressionable and obedient when provided with a legitimized ideology and social and institutional support, especially when it is done through coercive means by an authority." The Stanford Prison Study and the Milgram Experiment illustrate this.

Stanford Prison Study

In 1971, Psychology Professor Dr. Philip Zimbardo at Stanford University led a team of researchers in a study of the psychological effects of becoming a prisoner or guard. Twenty-four undergraduates were randomly selected to play either a guard or a prisoner.

The guards easily adapted to their role using inhumane techniques to degrade and destroy their wards. So brutal were the techniques used that five of the prisoners quit the experiment early and the entire study was stopped early (much to the chagrin of the guards).

The experimenters said, "Approximately one-third of the guards exhibited sadistic tendencies. Most of the guards were upset when the experiment concluded early. The prisoners also internalized their roles and grew increasingly passive and depressive." The study concludes that the "situation caused the participants' behaviors, rather than anything inherent in their individual personalities."

This study validates the Milgram experiment, which found that the situation or culture can cause ". . . ordinary people without any hostility on their part, [to] become agents in a terrible destructive process." The film The Experimenter, which had a limited commercial and VOD release in fall of 2015, received universally good reviews and portrayed the life and experiments of Dr. Milgram.

The Milgram Experiment

In July of 1961, after the trial of German Nazi war criminal Adolf Eichmann, Stanley Milgram, a Yale University psychologist, conducted a series of experiments to measure "the willingness of the study participants to obey a figure of authority, who instructed them to perform acts that conflicted with their personal conscience." Milgram summarized the experiment in his 1973 *Harper's Magazine* article, "The Perils of Obedience," writing:

"The legal and philosophic aspects of obedience are of enormous importance, but they say very little about how most people behave in concrete situations. I set up a simple experiment at Yale University to test how much pain an ordinary citizen would inflict on another person simply because he was ordered to by an experimental scientist. Stark authority was pitted against the subjects' (participants') strongest moral imperatives against hurting others, and, with the subjects' (participants') ears ringing with the screams of the targets, authority won more often than not. The extreme willingness of adults to go to any lengths on the command of an authority constitutes the chief finding of the study and the fact most urgently demanding explanation.

". . . ordinary people, simply doing their jobs, without any particular hostility on their part, can become agents in a terrible destructive process. Moreover, even when the destructive effects of their work become patently clear and they are asked to carry out actions incompatible with fundamental standards or morality, relatively few people have the resources needed to resist authority."

Bridgegate, the scandal surrounding New Jersey Governor and former presidential candidate Chris Christie, is more about the culture in Christie's administration than the irresponsible, vindictive and retaliatory actions of his closest aides and allies in the Port Authority when they crippled traffic in Fort Lee, New Jersey, for four days in September 2013. Christie has forcefully asserted "I am not a bully" and claims not to have been aware or involved. While there is not yet a smoking gun linking him directly to the incident, Christie does have a reputation for being retaliatory and a bully; therefore, I am doubtful that he was not aware, even if he was not involved. If he was not aware or involved, there is clearly a culture in his administration that condones and encourages this type of action.

David Gergen, who is senior political analyst for CNN and has served as an advisor to four U.S. presidents, used Richard Nixon and Watergate as an analogy, indicating that while, perhaps, they did not know or were not directly involved, they created a climate where their staffs did what they would want. Christie, like Nixon, is a micro-manager who wants to be aware of everything, calling into question the extent of his involvement.

CASE STUDY

From Canada's national symbol to Canada's national shame—The Royal Canadian Mounted Police (RCMP)— An example of a Dictatorial culture

The image of a police officer on a horse in a scarlet coat and wide-brimmed hat is Canada's most recognized symbol. Established in 1864, the Mounties evolved into a hugely complex police force with close to 30,000 employees.

Once an international icon of solid Canadian Values, the RCMP has found itself mired in a litany of organizational, legal and political controversies. In July 2010, the Canadian Broadcasting Service, in a documentary called Mounties Under Fire, described them as having a "broken culture."

The RCMP addresses its core values:

"Recognizing the dedication of all employees, we will create and maintain an environment of individual safety, well-being and development. We are guided by:

- Integrity
- Honesty

- Professionalism
- Compassion
- Respect
- Accountability."

When I look at their history since 1978, the RCMP demonstrates serious organizational problems with most of the characteristics of a Dictatorial culture. What really stands out most are the denials, cover-ups and efforts to "keep it in the family."

In 2003, a scandal surrounded the administration of the force's pension and insurance plans due to allegations of fraud and abuse during the outsourcing of the plans, so the Federal Government appointed an independent investigator. While the scandal was sufficiently significant to taint the force, the review highlighted a fundamental flaw in the culture: rather than encourage disclosure of wrongdoing, senior management retaliated against employees who brought the issues forward. The investigator's report, titled "Restoring the Honour of the RCMP: December 2007," concluded "RCMP senior management allowed an unethical culture to develop, which discouraged the disclosing of wrongdoing and did not hold individuals to account for unethical behavior." This committee commended the people who were viewed as whistleblowers by senior management "as exemplifying the stated values of the RCMP, and those who subjected these people to reprisals expressed the exact opposite."

Professor Linda Duxbury of Carlton University in Ottawa conducted an extensive survey of RCMP members that found extreme frustration with managers. "What they were frustrated with was the top-down style of management, non-supportive managers who don't trust or respect their members, managers' inability to communicate effectively with staff, politically driven agendas, managers who are perceived to be careerists who are governed by their personal agendas and managers who do not walk the talk."

In the September 2007 issue of *Mcleans Canada*, a Sara Scott article asked: "Is this the end of the Toxic Boss? Judges are sending corporate bullies a message: treat your employees with respect." In the article, she highlights the RCMP, citing the case of Officer Nancy Sulz, a $50,000-per-year police officer with eight years experience who won nearly $1 million from the RCMP for being bullied by a senior officer.

Structured on a paramilitary model, the RCMP operated with a high degree of autonomy and independence until 2006, when the government finally recognized that the wrongdoing (which received a fair bit of media attention) could no longer be overlooked. A 2009 internal RCMP report, titled "RCMP Values—Driven Leadership" suggests that the workplace culture is badly in need of repair across the country and that some supervisors are "creating a toxic workplace, high levels of stress, and a culture of fear."

This report contains details about sick leave use for example. At the time of the report, 336 employees in British Columbia alone were on long-term disability, with some having been on leave for up to seven years. Health professionals estimate that 75 percent of those on sick leave suffer from Post Traumatic Stress Disorder "because of conflicts with supervisors and others within the organization."

In his book, *Inside the Secret World of Ottawa and the RCMP*, Paul Palango addresses the cult mentality. A highly regarded former officer describes it this way, "The RCMP resists any criticism, and it does not respect the public, bureaucrats, or politicians. If one of the brass gets involved in a controversy, there is no will within the force to assess the person's culpability. The saying is, 'Respect the rank, not the story.'" The book also details charges of abuse, assault, harassment and deceit that were routinely made to disappear.

The crisis within the RCMP hit a peak in July of 2010, when the Commissioner, William Elliott, was accused of being a bully by ten deputy and assistant commissioners who took their complaints directly to the Prime Minister's office. This was an unprecedented airing of dirty laundry for a notoriously insular organization.

Initially, the government decided to support Commissioner Elliott (the first civilian and first external commissioner) because they recognized that he was trying to change the toxic culture, and agreed with Elliott's assertion that those who were against the changes were trying to force him out (a classic tactical move by bullies). In the summer of 2011, the bullies won when Elliott resigned.

In November of 2011, Bob Paulson, a lifelong Mountie who promised to conduct a review of outstanding complaints of harassment, was appointed as the new commissioner. "Culture" was cited as the sixth issue in an article by Laura Payton and Alison Crawford titled "Seven Issues Facing the RCMP Commissioner" for the CBC News on October 27, 2011. "Mounties knew about it for years, but it was only through the publication of Brown's report that the general public learned about the RCMP's so-called penalty box culture where people who questioned authority were bullied, seconded to other government departments or sent on interminable French training."

Paulson has been challenged as a man of words only because of his failure to deliver on his commitment to positively change the culture to regain trust in the institution. His ability to make the promised changes is compromised by his dismissal of harassment claims and the efforts of some to unionize, as actions of a disgruntled minority.

In 2012, Staff Sergeant Gravelle, who was the Harassment, Human Rights and Alternative Dispute Resolution Coordinator for the Atlantic region, had to file a rights complaint herself because she was threatened with dismissal for filing complaints against her supervisor.

In October of 2013, Janet Merlo, a 20-year veteran RCMP Officer, wrote a book called *No One To Tell: Breaking My*

Silence on Life in the RCMP, in which she asserts that not much has changed since Paulson's appointment.

In September of 2014, an officer who suffered from Post Traumatic Stress Disorder, and was forced to retire, committed suicide. Family members claim that the force does not do enough to address the stigma of mental illness and a recent audit found that close to 40 percent of RCMP employees who are on long-term disability, cite mental health problems.

As of February 2016, little seems to have changed. Fresh allegations have emerged about severe sexual harassment—also not reported until long after the fact because of fear of reprisals—in the Canadian Police College Explosives Unit dating back several years.

Paulson launched a review, but is limiting investigations to specific reported cases rather than implement a systemic review of the RCMP culture. The CBC reported that "While there may be serious, individual cases that would merit independent investigation, overall, he said he sees no need for an external body to handle the vast majority of harassment complaints."

The CBC further reported: Ian McPhail, Chair of the Civilian Complaints and Review Commission for the RCMP, is eager to see how well the RCMP is dealing with allegations of harassment. Reporting to a parliamentary commission in February 2016, he said he asked Paulson for an update four months earlier on how the Mounties have implemented his recommendations but never heard back. Last month, the Minister of Public Safety asked the commission to conduct a follow-up review.

Nothing short of a systemic organization-wide review, along with extensive managerial housecleaning, will change the culture, which is so embedded, it has survived at every level despite years of internal investigations and complaints.

The Disjointed Culture

The Disjointed culture can best be described as a loose federation. It tries to accommodate everyone. Like a Dictatorial culture, it is hierarchical and bureaucratic, and process is a substitute for purpose. Usually, departments and regional locations operate in silos. There are few checks and balances and bullies can, and do, operate freely. Here, as in the Dictatorial, bullies are usually considered high performers and heroes. Bystanders, and those who are bullied, do not trust the systems in place to report abuse because of fear of exposure and retaliation.

Characteristics of a Disjointed culture:

- There is a lack of structure and discipline.

- Rules are not consistently applied.

- Events are reactionary.

- Rituals are substitutes for core values.

- There is a cover-up mentality.

- There is a lack of alignment to purpose, values, operating principles, vision and initiatives (usually because there are none or too many).

- There is ambiguity and subjectivity in performance management (metrics, rewards, recognition and advancement).

- Cronyism and nepotism are evident.

- It is highly emotional and reactionary.

- Best practice, state-of-the-art employment policies are evident, but, in practice, nonexistent.

- Leaders live with false delusions.

- People are allowed to discredit others.

- Where there are multiple locations, it is a loose federation of companies operating in silos.

- Turf is jealously guarded.

- There is little to no transparency.

- There are no checks and balances.

The Catholic Church—An Example of a Disjointed Culture

John Thavis, in his book *The Vatican Diaries*, provides a behind-the-scenes look at the power, personalities, and politics at the heart of the Catholic Church. This book was published just before the resignation of Pope Benedict XVI.

The Vatican that Pope Francis inherited has a culture that is disjointed and dysfunctional.

It is encouraging to witness the new Pope's recognition that the Catholic Church needs to restore its reputation for being a respected defender of human rights, peace, and social justice. To do this, he must initiate a cultural transformation. The Pope's comments on gay priests, the senior appointments he has made, and his resolve to change the Vatican Bank are great indicators of necessary changes.

Although the initial words and actions are positive, it is yet to be seen whether Pope Francis can break the stronghold of the hierarchy and the various autonomous orders. Being the first Pope from the Jesuit Order is a significant indicator, as the Jesuits more closely resemble what I define as a Stable culture with a reputation for rigidly instilling high ethical and moral standards with resolve and discipline.

On December 22, 2014, Pope Francis used his annual Christmas greeting to outline plans to fix the culture within the church. Holding back no punches, he scathingly criticized the culture and denounced those who "have sought power at the expense of others and those who have acted rigid, tough and arrogant."

And, as his papacy progresses, Pope Francis continues to appeal to the more progressive and inclusive wings of the Catholic Church. However, after four years of espoused openness, there has been little concrete action. As the traditionalists and the innovators wrestle for the church's future, Pope Francis remains both its linchpin and its weak link.

As Robert Mickens, editor-in-chief of Global Pulse, opined, "Up to this point, most of the Francis Revolution has been one of attitude and style. There's nothing at all wrong with that, but in Year Four of his pontificate those who are praying and pulling for Francis hope he starts making some substantial structural changes that are unassailable . . .

"If—God forbid!—the 79-year-old pope were to suddenly die, there is hardly anything he's done so far that a successor with a restorationist agenda could not undo, even without too much effort or controversy."

Two critical issues that innovators most hope he will address concretely are the role of women in the church and the sex abuse by clergy. While offering words of condolence and regret, there is little anyone can look to for real change. As always, change—real change—actionable change—begins at the top.

The Stable Culture

Values and beliefs are at the core of Stable cultures. People are the key component to the success of the organization. The Stable culture sets high, but reasonable, expectations; holds people accountable for performance, behaviors and actions; provides what is necessary for people to excel; fairness and equity rank high as values; and team trumps any individual recognition.

Characteristics of a Stable culture:

- There is a governance model in place that monitors more than the financials.

- There is a common and well-understood vision and purpose.

- Values and operating principles form a solid foundation.

- Rules (a code of conduct and terms of engagement) are simply stated and consistently applied.

- There is an effective and inclusive strategic planning process that proportionately focuses more on sustainable, long-term performance, and emphasizes agility to respond to ever-changing market conditions.

- All internal stakeholders are aligned with the plan, vision, values and operating principles.

- Roles, responsibilities and accountability are clearly defined.

- Vendor and government relations are positive and fair.

- A four-dimensional, balanced, measurement system is in place (customer, employee, financial and execution).

- The four R's are rigorously followed (doing the RIGHT things, the RIGHT way, by the RIGHT people at the RIGHT time).

- Competency and cooperation are modeled and encouraged.

- Team is valued over individual.

- People are taught to think.

- Employers know how employees feel.

- People are motivated to be all they can be.

- People are measured more by the quality of their contributions than the quantity of output and time spent.

- There is a clear value-exchange model in place (clear expectations of employees are set against what employees should expect from the organization).

- Bosses and subordinates have regular, equal conversations, during which the boss asks things such as "What do you need from me to deliver on what we have to achieve?"

- Leaders hear what they need to know.

- There is no fear of retaliation and people are comfortable in bringing forward ideas, issues and opportunities.

- Courage is highly valued.

- Mistakes are considered learning opportunities.

- There is a high level of transparency.

Best of all: doing the right thing pays off. ThyssenKrupp, one of the world's leading industrial manufacturers, cleaned house six years ago after a long history of corruption, internal strife and inefficiency. Heinrich Hiesinger was brought in as CEO to restructure the organization, and transform it into a culture of openness, integrity and reduced hierarchy.

Showing annual net profit and returning a dividend after just four years, ThyssenKrupp is looking forward to continued growth, solidification of core strengths and internal investment for long-term growth.

Summing up the transformation, Mr. Heisinger told the *Wall Street Journal*, "How could it happen that our company was maneuvering itself in such a difficult situation and nobody raised a hand or corrected it beforehand? We wanted to build an organization where hierarchy is strongly reduced, so that truth has a chance to move up from bottom to top."

CASE STUDY

On becoming a Stable culture— Shoppers Drug Mart (circa 1998-2008)

It is not unusual for subcultures to exist within an organization, i.e., where the overall culture is Dictatorial or Disjointed, and some departments or locations have Stable cultures; or conversely, where the corporate culture is Stable and some of the departments or locations are Dictatorial or Disjointed.

Having spent the bulk of my career in retail (twenty-three years with Loblaw Companies Ltd—Canada's largest food retailer—and ten years with Shoppers Drug Mart Corporation), overseeing in excess of one thousand locations, I have witnessed firsthand the dynamics of subcultures and the resulting effect on performance. At Shoppers Drug Mart, Canada's largest drug store chain, where I was a management partner for ten years, we built a positive high performance culture—what I refer to as a Stable culture.

In 1999, when we carried out a management-led buyout, we assessed that, while overall performance was respectable, it was not performing to its full potential. The market was growing at a faster rate than we were; there where inconsistencies across the chain in staffing levels, store conditions, pricing, hours of operation, in-stock positions, adherence to national programs. In essence, the only consistency was inconsistency.

Unfortunately, almost all of the senior management team had to be replaced—they had the technical capability but, as they fundamentally disagreed with the massive change that was required, we recognized early on that we needed a team that bought into the plan.

Glenn Murphy, someone I worked with at Loblaw's, was hired as chair and CEO.

The new team we selected, with a few exceptions, was promoted from within. We chose well, as they became one of the most aligned, driven, and cohesive teams I have had the pleasure of working with.

Immediately following the buyout, we embarked on a program to totally transform the organization. The first step was to conduct a cultural assessment of the corporate and regional offices, followed by an assessment of all store locations.

Poor and marginally performing stores were benchmarked against comparable high performers. What we found was that most of the high-performing stores had the characteristics of a Stable culture and most of the poor and marginal performers had the characteristics of Dictatorial or Disjointed cultures. Bullying was evident in many of the corporate departments, the regional offices, and in the store locations that had the characteristics of Dictatorial and Disjointed cultures.

In tangible terms, we found the high performance stores had sustainable financial results; lower employment costs; higher customer satisfaction scores; lower staff attrition; higher sales per square foot; higher sales per transaction; higher in-stock positions and higher inventory turns; and a higher sell-through of seasonal items. We also heard directly from our customers. Because of the inconsistencies in our offerings and their shopping experiences, we were "over-promising and under-delivering."

To realize full potential, we needed to significantly increase store count and operating hours, including additional 24-hour locations, extended hours and opening on Sundays and holidays.

A huge challenge was our reliance on pharmacists. Under Canadian legislation, drug stores cannot open, even for an hour, without a pharmacist on site. When we hired new pharmacists, it was like pouring water into a bucket with a big hole in the bottom. The attrition rate was over 30 percent and the vacancy run rate was just over 20 percent. To add to the dilemma, there was a worldwide shortage of pharmacists at the time. This alone was sufficient reason to go through a cultural transformation—ensuring all locations had a Stable one. To reach our growth objectives, we needed to become an "Employer of Choice."

The transformation was complete within a year. It was hard work and we initially met with significant resistance at all levels. We cut through a lot of it by distinguishing what people disliked about the proposed changes against what they disagreed with because they felt it was fundamentally wrong. We made the point that, "because you don't like or agree with something, does not mean it is wrong—it may be different than what you would like or do, but it is not necessarily wrong." Making this distinction, and only debating what they fundamentally disagreed with versus what they did not like, allowed us to move quickly. Many organizational transformations are derailed because of resisters who feel the changes will erode their autonomy or power.

After our cultural transformation, the entire network of stores performed more consistently. In fact, the overall performance of the organization dramatically improved—specifically, within five years the number of stores doubled, our EPS went from less than $1 to $2.64, the enterprise value went from $5 per share to $58, we became the "employer of choice" and the attrition and vacancy rate for pharmacists went to a low single digit.

Throughout my career as a manager and executive, creating positive, high-performing cultures has been critical to my success and, by extension, the employees I was responsible for, and the organizations I represented.

During and since the release of my book, *The Bully's Trap: Bullying in the Workplace*, I have received a lot of pushback from executives who discount the value of a positive culture and consider cultural initiatives as human resources gobbledygook. I do agree that, when cultural initiatives are not tied to performance, it usually is gobbledygook.

Throughout the 2016 U.S. political election season, we are witnessing on prime time a Cultural Revolution against political establishment, largely because the mood and emotions of the nation have been misread. Based on interviews with more than six hundred people on bullying in the workplace, I can assert that board directors and senior leadership are similarly misreading the mood and emotions of their employees. Unfortunately, all too many don't care.

Evidence of this is the release of the "World's Most Admired Companies" in the March 28, 2016, issue of *Fortune* magazine. Fortune partnered with Korn Ferry and the Hay Group (both human resources experts), and asked thousands of insiders, directors and analysts to pick the most respected names in global business. It is unlikely that non-executive employees were asked. If they were, rather than landing as number three on the list, it is unlikely that Amazon would have even made it.

Late last year, the *New York Times* published a scathing article on Amazon's culture referenced elsewhere here. This February, in Seattle, I interviewed a number of current and former Amazon employees who validated the allegations made in the NYT article. What was described to me was a rats' nest of toxicity where only "narcissistic, psychopathic bullies thrive and survive." Amazon's third place on the list challenges the credibility of the report because it misrepresents what customers, prospective employees and investors should know about each company.

In February, the Faas Foundation and the Yale Center for Emotional Intelligence announced a joint initiative—"Emotion Revolution in the Workplace"—to scientifically determine how employees feel about their work, why they feel the way they do, and the quantifiable effects these emotions have on individual and organizational performance, as well as health and well-being.

What we already know, according to Gallup polling, is that more than 70 percent of North American workers are not engaged. More significantly, a study that appeared in *Management Science* in February 2016 concluded that over 120,000 deaths may be attributable to workplace stress. Understanding and accepting indisputable evidence that shows how emotions influence performance is the prerequisite step to creating positive, high-performance cultures.

Early in my career, a mentor suggested I meet on a regular basis with everyone I was responsible for to understand how they felt about their work, why they felt the way they did, whether they felt they were contributing to their full potential, and what prevented them from being able to do so. This helped me understand performance motivators and restrainers. With this information, I was able to respond to employees' desires to be positively challenged; to not be distracted by, or involved in, non-value-added activities; and reduce unnecessary stress factors.

Over the years, using this method, a cultural model evolved, which was anchored by a value exchange covenant based on the ethic of reciprocity. Any organization, team or individual can apply this model. In summary, this is how it works:

- First—Determine what the organization expects from the employee.

- Second—Test the reasonableness of the expectations.

- Third—Determine what the employee needs to be able to deliver on the organization's expectations.

- Fourth—Reach agreement on what each expects from the other—"The Covenant."

- Fifth—Initiate regular and ongoing discussions on the efficacy of The Covenant.

Developing this model requires a rigorous review of almost every factor involved in organizational dynamics. In most cases, it will challenge how organizations are governed and organized; how they make decisions, hire, fire, promote, motivate, communicate, measure, reward, recognize, align, as well as distribute assignments; identify and handle risk; and handle crisis.

From my research, and from what we are likely to find in the "Emotion Revolution in the Workplace," we know that fear of being let go is one of the biggest concerns that employees have. When I identify this in organizations I work with, the usual reaction is, "Surely they don't expect us to provide a guarantee of employment?" I respond to this by indicating that employees understand market dynamics, but are looking to their employer's commitment to use job cuts as a last resort, rather than a knee-jerk reaction when short-term targets are not met.

They also expect fairness and humane treatment when cuts are made. To illustrate how not to respond, I now reference Melissa Mayer, the CEO of Yahoo, and how, in trying to quell discontent, she called an all-hands meeting to declare, "The days of bloodletting are over." Less than two weeks later, she demanded the firing of another thousand employees in a desperate attempt to save her own skin. Her future and her reputation could have been saved had she said something to the effect, "We have gone through a tough time. I know the toll it has taken on employees, I also have to be realistic that we will go through more difficult times. But, let me assure you that I will do everything I can to minimize the negative effect on employees and, if further cuts are required, we will do it in a consistently fair and humane manner."

What I am proposing here may not be as sexy as the kind of perks being used by a number of organizations to attract and retain talent. However, it is a more effective and sustainable motivational method of responding to how employees want to feel: helping to create positive, high performance cultures.

Altering the Attitudes of Organizational Leaders

Organizational leaders' attitudes regarding bullying in the workplace is the single most important determiner as to whether an organization is free and safe from bullying.

If leadership does not understand what constitutes bullying and is unaware of the consequences to the individual, organization and the community, bullying may be condoned, and even encouraged.

Worse, if leadership believes that bullying is an effective tactic to achieve results, bullying will certainly be condoned and encouraged.

If the CEO is also the CBO (Chief Bullying Officer), bullying will not only be condoned and encouraged; managers throughout the organization will also be expected to bully.

It's challenging, if not impossible, to change an organization—any organization—if leadership doesn't take responsibility and isn't held accountable. After scandalous reports of falsifications, cover-ups and even deaths, the Veterans Administration's new head Robert McDonald pledged to "transform" the agency in 2014. Since then, not one senior-level executive has been fired, internal beneficiaries of fraud are still employed and whistle-blowers are not protected. VA leaders are letting down veterans as well as the people it hired to serve those veterans.

Corporate cultures that discourage employee reports of wrongdoing are ticking time bombs. I've cited numerous organizations where bosses either condoned wrongdoing or made it impossible for employees to report it. These issues demonstrate that creating a psychologically healthy workplace isn't just in the interest of employees—it's another form of risk management for CEOs who want to avoid becoming the next Volkswagen, for example.

Regulations Aren't Sufficient: Leadership Determines Outcomes

And, for some industries, the issues are endemic to the larger industry's culture. Labaton Sucharow, in conjunction with the University of Notre Dame, delivered an explosive and revealing report in 2015 on the financial services industry in "The Street, The Bull and The Crisis." The findings reveal that cheating is still pervasive despite extensive efforts by regulators, and whistle-blowing is unlikely, if not impossible.

Findings reveal the depth of the problem . . .

Forty-seven percent of respondents believe that competitors have engaged in unethical or illegal activity to gain an advantage.

This figure jumps to 51 percent for individuals earning $500,000 or more per year.

More than one-third (34 percent) of those earning $500,000 or more annually have first-hand knowledge of wrongdoing in the workplace.

Twenty-seven percent of those surveyed disagree that the financial services industry puts the best interests of clients first. This figure rises to 38 percent for those earning $500,000 or more per year.

. . . and the inadequacy of the solutions

Twenty-eight percent of respondents earning $500,000 or more per year say their company's confidentiality policies and procedures bar them from reporting potentially illegal or unethical activities directly to law enforcement or regulatory authorities.

Twenty-five percent of respondents earning $500,000 or more annually have signed or been asked to sign a confidentiality agreement that would prohibit reporting illegal or unethical activities to authorities.

Nineteen percent of respondents believe their employer would retaliate if they were to report wrongdoing in the workplace.

To understand the mindset of organizational leaders on bullying, 138 leaders were interviewed—72 CEOs, 26 executive directors, and 40 board chairs across Canada and the United States. Thirty-three of the 138 were women.

These leaders represent a cross-section of organizations, private and public, government, health care, manufacturing, financial services, retail, technology, transportation and resources. All but 21 of the organizations had multiple locations and the number of employees ranged from a low of just under 400 to a high of 64,000. Employees in 16 of the organizations were represented by a union or an association.

The methodology used was a structured, but open-ended, face-to-face discussion with each to gain qualitative insights. I do not claim this to be a scientific study; however, the findings and observations validate, and are consistent with, the findings and observations on the interviews conducted with more than 300 people who either have been bullied or are close to someone who has been bullied.

Most of the interviewed leaders debated what constituted bullying. Most would not accept the proposed definition and viewed what I described as bullying as more simply an aggressive management style. All did acknowledge, however, that sexual and racial harassment was wrong and should be considered bullying. These debates at the front end of the discussion gave context to the larger discussions. While most felt my definition was extreme, all but a few accepted it for the purpose of the discussion.

The purpose was to gain an understanding of their attitudes and level of awareness, so the interviews avoided debating the rightness or wrongness of bullying.

The findings

1. The overall level of awareness and understanding of what constitutes bullying (and what does not) is low. Most of the managers I interviewed do not view bullying as workplace violence.

2. Although most want their organizations to be viewed as employers of choice and rate brand and reputation value as a high priority, few view bullying as a business risk in their organization.

3. There is a low overall level of awareness and understanding of the impact that bullying has on the individual, organization and community.

4. When given our definition of bullying and the ways and means of bullying, all but seventeen indicated that they, at some point in their careers, have been targeted. Ironically, many described their experiences and those of others they are close to with great indignation.

5. Seventy-three percent of the CEOs indicated that they could argue they were being bullied by their Board of Directors because of the pressure for short-term results.

6. All but three of the executive directors of the not-for-profit organizations indicated that they spend a disproportionate amount of their time dealing with unreasonably difficult board members.

7. Sixty-seven percent acknowledged that they use bullying as a tactic to get things done, improve productivity and/or get better deals.

8. Sixty-nine percent believe that those who are targeted have performance or attitudinal issues. Therefore, with the exception of sexual or racial bullying, it is warranted.

9. Seventy-one percent condone bullying because they believe that fear is a better motivator than what they refer to as "that human resources stuff."

10. The notion that bullying causes targets to reduce their level of engagement, commitment and performance was widely rejected.

11. Fifty-two percent of the leaders who operate where there is workplace violence and/or anti-bullying legislation were aware of the legislation. Those who were aware felt that their organizations were compliant and only seven percent could describe what "compliant" meant.

12. Eighty-six percent indicated that they would not educate their employees on bullying because of a concern that employees would use bullying as a sword or a shield when they are subject to disciplinary action.

13. While 62 percent indicated that they had stated values and operating principles, only 14 percent of the sixty-two could recite what they were.

14. Only 27 percent could give adequate answers to cultural indicators that could reveal bullying is occurring, such as high turnover.

15. Of the 40 board chairs interviewed, six indicated their boards reviewed some of the indicators that there could be a cultural problem.

16. Fifty-four percent measure success beyond the financials and 44 percent of this group uses a balanced scorecard methodology.

17. Of the 34 who had to deal with instances of bullying, only four found the alleged bully to be at fault.

18. Sixty-nine percent considered staff turnover as a positive as it "gets rid of dead weight" and "allows for new blood."

19. Fifty-one percent acknowledged that employees in their organizations may be afraid to report wrongdoings.

20. Eighty-six percent felt that whistleblowers should be required to absolutely prove the allegation.

21. Fifty-two percent consider whistleblowers treasonous.

22. Sixty-three percent recognized that they may not be hearing what they need to hear.

23. Seventy-six percent indicated that they often accept one-sided representations when there is a conflict or disagreement.

24. Seventy-one percent feel it is healthy to create a certain amount of conflict because "it makes people competitive."

25. Thirty-two percent manage by "walking around."

26. Twenty-four percent used the latest economic downturn to "clean house." Most of this group challenged their managers to force people out rather than lay them off.

Based on the work I have done in the area and my analysis of interviews conducted, it is my assessment that:

- Management doesn't consider bullying to be an issue.

- More than half of the organizational leaders are bullies.

- Because of the pressure to deliver on short-term results, most organizational leaders condone and encourage bullying to force productivity and force people out.

- Organizational leaders' attitudes on bullying beget bullies throughout organizations. Bullies become the heroes and the bullied become not only the targets, but also the villains (bullied bullies).

- As long as results are achieved, Boards of Directors are not interested in whether or not bullying goes on.

- Organizational leaders view fear as a more effective motivator than performance management systems.

- Workplace violence and anti-bullying legislation is viewed as an unnecessary aggravation that is relegated to either Legal or Human Resources to fulfill the bare minimum of what's required.

- Short of a "going postal" situation, bullying will not be considered an issue with most organizational leaders.

- There is a fear that raising the level of awareness on bullying will create abuse with employees accusing managers of bullying when they try to correct deficiencies, and managers will become afraid to manage.

The scandal at Rutgers University illustrates the attitudes of organizational leadership on bullying

In the fall of 2012, a video showed Mike Rice, The Scarlet Kings men's basketball coach, verbally and physically abusing players. Rutgers President Robert L. Barchi was made aware of the video in November of 2012, but claims he did not view it. An ethics committee made up of board members and trustees did view it at a December 14 meeting and were satisfied that the three-game suspension Rice received was adequate.

Barchi, in defending his role, placed blame on Athletic Director Tim Pernetti and other officials, saying they decided to follow a process involving university lawyers, human resource professionals, and outside counsel. This is based on a commissioned report recommending that Rice be suspended and sent to an anger management course.

The 50-page report, compiled by an outside lawyer, made clear that Rice's outbursts "were not isolated" and that "he had a fierce temper, used homophobic and misogynistic slurs, kicked his players and threw basketballs at them." The report went on to describe him as "passionate, energetic and demanding," and claimed that his behaviors constituted "permissible training," and he "caused them to play better during the team's basketball games."

After the video exploded in the media, Barchi had Rice fired. One can only assume the firing was in reaction to the disastrous publicity—not Rice's behavior!

I assert: if this case does not prompt leaders to view workplace bullying differently, nothing will.

One organization's experience doesn't seem to provide sufficient warning to other organizations, even those in related fields.

In January, the *New York Times* reported on the World Anti-Doping Agency's (WADA) report on corruption and possible criminal behavior at the management level of the International Association of Athletics Federations—the world's governing body of track and field and its apparent endorsement of its president, Sebastian Coe, about whom there have been whispers of affiliations with people involved with doping.

"With so much corruption in international sports, there would be no guarantee that Coe's successor would be blemish-free." Using this as a rationalization to keep Sebastian Coe as the head of the International Association of Athletics Federations is like saying you'll let the fox guard the henhouse to avoid involving wolves. According to the WADA report, it's impossible that he could have been unaware of the corruption. In fact, there's a good chance he was involved in the corruption. That they can't find one clean sports official to put in charge of the IAAF is a shameful message to send to our youth, who are growing up in a world where trust has been eroded in nearly every aspect of society.

When the Going Gets Tough, the Bullied Go

There has been much debate on the Miami Dolphins harassment situation. In October of 2013, Jonathan Martin walked away from a multimillion-dollar contract with the Miami Dolphins alleging harassment by his teammates, coach, and in particular, the ring leader Richie Incognito. Incognito, who has a record of abusive behavior, claimed he was asked by the coaching team to "toughen him [Martin] up."

Many feel that what happened to Martin was appropriate as football is a tough game and, if players can't take the heat, they should get out. I counter this argument using boot camps in the military as an analogy. There is no question that it would be irresponsible not to test and train soldiers for physical and emotional endurance, and the intent of boot camps is to strengthen individuals before they are sent into harm's way.

My analysis of what happened to Martin is that Incognito's intention and tactics were to destroy rather than strengthen.

In conditioning people to work in dangerous or tough environments, the use of racial and homophobic slurs, threats, innuendoes and demanding questionable actions effectively weaken targets to the point they want out which, in my view, is what happened to Martin. The National Football League's independent investigators found that this is a cultural issue within the Miami Dolphins largely due to the attitude of the coaching and management team.

"THAT'S NOT THE AMAZON I KNOW."

In the summer of 2015, *The New York Times* printed an extensive report on the challenge of working at Amazon. While rumors—and many facts—had long swirled around working conditions in its warehouses (e.g., ambulances lined up and regularly dispatched outside a Pennsylvania facility with no air conditioning at the height of summer), this report detailed conditions of Amazon's managerial workers versus its blue collar staff.

From public performance reviews to intolerance of illness, pregnancy, parenthood or any other personal diversion from work, the story portrayed a work environment in which one worker claimed, "Nearly every person

I worked with I saw cry at their desk." Dubbed
"Purposeful Darwinism," some HR executives
confirmed the stories, while official responses
deny the claims.

Glassdoor, a jobs website that collects
employee reviews of corporate environments,
seems to support a less-than-favorable work
environment–only about two-thirds of employees would recommend working there to a
friend, despite the cushy salaries and blue-chip
name. Why would anyone work at a place that
drove its employees so hard they couldn't vaca-
tion, tend to aging parents, have a baby, enjoy
a free weekend or ignore middle-of-the-night
work emails? In a word: Money. It's the most
powerful of all motivators and cudgels, proving that toxic work environments come in many
colors and one of them is green.

Jeff Bezos' response to the *New York Times*
article, "That's not the Amazon I know," only
illustrates his lack of awareness of the reality–or it is a calculated PR move to mitigate
the culture he built so carefully. Rather than
address the issues revealed in the *NY Times*
expose, Bezos and his PR executive Jay Carney
(former White House Press Secretary) went
on a witchhunt to find out who talked to the
reporter.

Bullying and Board Governance

"Good governance does not just prevent misdeeds
but actually improves the corporation."
–RAM CHARAN

How accountable are Boards of Directors for bullying that occurs in organizations they govern? As governance models evolve, there is no clear answer. An easier question is: Should boards be held accountable when bullying occurs and should they be responsible for ensuring that people in the organization are free and safe from bullying? I assert they should be. Bullying in the workplace exposes an organization to risk. Boards are responsible for protecting and growing value for the shareholder, so anything that puts the brand or its reputation at risk, puts the enterprise value at risk.

The scandalous frauds and abuses at Nortel and others left gaping holes in the checks and balances intended to keep corporations honest and protect stakeholders, which resulted in massive bankruptcies, cheated investors out of billions, caused massive layoffs and destroyed whole communities.

The primary role of a board is strategy formulation and policymaking. Their value, however, is reduced when they do not consider their accountability for how the strategy and policies are implemented.

Along with the failure of oversight mechanisms, this exposes directors to considerable litigation risk, as they are, de facto, the first and last defense for fiduciary responsibility. Whether boards are let down by management, or they are asleep at the wheel, they must step up as major reforms are essential.

In *Money for Nothing*, John Gillespie and David Zweig describe the failure of corporate boards and expose the flaws of a dysfunctional system. While the focus of the book is on shareholder rights, the authors recognize other stakeholders by advocating: "In modern economic thinking, boards should also monitor the interests of employees, customers, suppliers, creditors and the communities and the environment in which a firm operates, because these interests can be critical to increasing the long-term value of the shareholders' investment." For many, this can also include communities affected by local employment, environmental hazards or the exploitation of natural resources.

The suicide of Pierre Wauthier, CFO of Zurich Insurance Group AG, in August of 2013, highlights the risk of a toxic culture, with investor confidence shaken alongside suggestions that Wauthier was subject to excessive pressure. After the suicide, the company announced that the board was launching a cultural review. According to board governance guru Ram Charan, in his books *Owning Up* and *Boards That Deliver*, good governance does not just prevent misdeeds, but actually improves the corporation.

Governance now means leadership, and gone are the days when board members would ceremoniously sit on boards, gathering prestige, and ensuring the company was in compliance with the rules and regulations of the industry. To highlight the mission of progressive boards, Charan quotes Andy Grove, founder, former CEO and Chair of Intel: "[A progressive board aims] to ensure that the success of a company is longer lasting than any CEO's reign, than any market opportunity, than any product cycle."

In analyzing organizations that have had a reversal of fortune, and those that have gone down, a major factor was the profile of the CEO. The CEOs were often also CBOs. Many have argued that there was no way to see the subprime mortgage crisis coming. We now know there were those who did, who blew the whistle, but were not heard because of CBOs who would not allow voices of dissent to be heard. Too many CBOs see the organization as an extension of their own egos. This usually results in a hostile and toxic culture that costs companies dearly in lost productivity and intellectual capital and has caused the downfall of many organizations. The question that must be asked here is: Where were the directors?"

Lehman Brothers and AIG are two good examples of companies that could have survived and prospered with better governance. On a much larger scale, the global financial meltdown could have been avoided had there been better governance.

Lehman Brothers was a storied institution that survived two World Wars, the Great Depression, and practically every other calamity in its 158-year history, but was brought down in the largest bankruptcy by their CEO Richard Fuld, also known as "the Gorilla." Many blame his bullying as the direct cause of Lehman's downfall. Fuld bullied everyone around him and created a culture of fear and intimidation to the extent that even the Lehman directors were afraid of him. The longest tenured CEO on Wall Street, Fuld kept his job as the subprime mortgage crisis took hold, while CEOs of other institutions were forced to resign. The Lehman board remained reluctant to challenge Fuld as the firm's share price spiraled lower and lower.

In his book, *A Colossal Failure of Common Sense*, insider Lawrence G. McDonald had this to say: "King Richard had even turned Lehman's Board of Directors into a kind of largely irrelevant lower chamber. This was yet another group to rubberstamp his decisions and collect generous fees. It was not for supplying well-meant and lucid wisdom in the current wild marketplace, but for agreeing with the monarch, accepting his all-knowing take on the bank's investments. Above all, the board was not to rock the royal barge as it made its steady way down the stream."

Given the number of jobs lost and portfolios savaged, it's clear the effect of one bad boss may be felt far beyond the walls of a single corporation. "Joe Cassano: The Man Who Crashed the World," as he was labeled by Michael Lewis in the August 2009 feature in *Vanity Fair*, may be responsible for bringing AIG, the U.S. economy, and the global financial system to their knees.

Cassano was widely known as a bully across AIG, where the view of him was consistent: "a guy with a crude feel for financial risk, but a real talent for bullying people who doubted him."

"AIG became a dictatorship," says one London trader. "Joe would bully people around. He'd humiliate them." As with Lehman Brothers, where was the board in all of this? Afraid and negligent.

Notwithstanding all of the board reform that has occurred since the financial meltdown, relatively little has changed in how boards function. Unfortunately, it is still an old boys' club where there is not a proper balance of power and control, checks and balances. I assert that, if there were, we would not be hearing the almost daily horrendous stories in the media about abuse of power, corruption and greed, which continue to put our economies and society at risk.

Below, you might find helpful my previous discussion on bullying at the board level—which speaks directly to this issue.

Bullying: One of the Greatest Risks to the Organization

Originally published in *Directors & Boards Magazine*, 2016 First Quarter Issues

Rarely a day goes by when there is not a story in the media about abuse of power, inappropriate behavior, and corruption and greed on the part of leadership in every segment of our society worldwide. Whether it is business, industry, government, military, police services, education, law, social services, health care, sports, journalism, media or religion, none have been immune.

Where this occurs in organizations, there almost always exists a culture of bullying and fear.

In my book *The Bully's Trap*, I assert that, just as boards are responsible for protecting and growing enterprise value for the shareholder, they must also be responsible for ensuring that all other stakeholders are free and safe from bullying, because bullying is one of the greatest risks to the organization.

Volkswagen has suffered a huge loss in its brand and reputation value, which has translated into a huge loss in its enterprise value that could be fatal. Most assume that the emissions scandal is the cause. I argue that the cause is the result of a culture that has condoned and encouraged wrongdoing. Even more problematic is bullying employees to engage in and/or witness the wrongdoings, and threatening severe retaliation against those in a position to expose the situation. It is interesting to note that the scandal was reported following a power play at the board level, which exposed a severely fractured, negatively political and dysfunctional board.

The scandalous frauds and abuses, which have become the norm, usually reveal gaping holes in the checks and balances that should be in place to keep organizations honest, and to safely protect stakeholders. Poor corporate governance has ruined organizations, and threatened economies and governments. This has resulted in calls for board reform.

More and more common are activist shareholders who bully boards and CEOs to force change that often runs counter to the direction, strategy and values of the organization, and may not be in the best interest of other stakeholders and the sustainability of the organization. In what I refer to as the continuum of bullying, most of the bullying starts off at the top and is usually the result of focusing on short-term vs. long-term results. If the board wants to focus on the short term, they usually bully the CEO into compliance, who in turn bullies his or her direct reports, who then bully theirs. Most of these bullied bullies, and in turn their targets, become bullies at home. In turn, most of the children of these bullied bullies develop social disorders resulting in what I believe to be the biggest social issue of our generation.

In their book *Money for Nothing* (Free Press 2010), John Gillespie and David Zweig describe the failure of corporate boards and expose the flaws of a dysfunctional system. While the focus of the book is on shareholder rights, the authors recognize the other stakeholders by advocating, "In modern economic thinking boards should monitor the interests of employees, customers, suppliers, creditors and the communities and the environments in which a firm operates, because these interests can be critical to increasing the long-term value of the shareholder investment."

A *New York Times* article, "Integrity Takes a Toll at the Port Authority" by Jim Dwyer, tells the story of Patrick J. Foye, the executive director of the Port Authority of New York and New Jersey. Foye, who, rather than being supported by David Sampson, the chair of the Port Authority, was retaliated against by him because Foye did the right thing in putting a stop to the politically motivated actions now known as Bridgegate. The article reported that Foye "under oath told a story that provided the first clear view of near gangsterism at the top levels. . . ."

The August 2013 suicide of Pierre Wauthier, the CEO of Zurich Insurance, has highlighted the highest risk of a toxic culture. In a suicide note, Wauthier said that the chair of the board, Josef Ackermann, "had created an unbearable working environment." The suicide resulted in Ackermann leaving Zurich, and exposed other questionable activities and practices at Zurich.

In analyzing organizations that have had reversals of fortune, and those that have gone down, a major factor has been the profile of the CEO. In most cases, the CEO was also the CBO (Chief Bullying Officer). Many have argued that there was no way to see the subprime mortgage crisis coming. We now know there were those who did, and who blew the whistle, but were not heard because of the CEOs who would not allow voices of dissent to be heard. CBOs view the organizations they run as extensions of their narcissistic selves. These CEOs not only bully those under them but also the boards over them.

Lehman Brothers and AIG are two examples of companies that could have survived and prospered if they had had the benefit of a strong board and better governance. On a much larger scale, the global financial meltdown could have been avoided had there been better governance.

A ruthless abuse of power

As a board advisor, the most bizarre and outrageous case I have ever encountered was a CEO who spied on all of his board and executives to find dirt on them. At one retreat, he facilitated prostitutes to service select members of the board and executives, all of which was recorded. All of this was done to extort from them their blind loyalty and obedience. The CEO made sure that everyone he had something on knew that he had this card. Those who were clean and did not succumb to the pimping were aggressively bullied to the point that most of them quit. Gaining absolute power, he ruthlessly used and abused it. Where it not for the courage of an executive who became aware of this and blew the whistle, this monster would still be wreaking havoc.

Notwithstanding all of the board reform that has occurred since the financial meltdown, relatively little has changed in how boards function. Unfortunately it is still an old boys' club where there is not a proper balance of power and control, checks and balances. I assert that if there were, we would not be hearing the almost daily horrendous stories in the media about abuse of power, corruption and greed, which continue to put our economies and society at risk.

Human Resources—
Part of the Problem or Part of the Solution?

When I go into organizations to do an assessment, it is usually when the organization is in serious trouble or after a major incident. The first thing I attempt to determine is the role that Human Resources plays in influencing culture.

In many organizations, and with many of the cases that I have dealt with, I have found that well over three-quarters of the time, Human Resources is part of the problem versus part of the solution.

In most cases, human resource people view bullying as a personality clash or a management style issue and apply conflict resolution techniques to resolve the problem. Usually, this makes the situation worse for the target and the bully feels further empowered because s/he has successfully deflected his or her predatory behaviors, manipulating Human Resources to become an ally.

In Disjointed cultures, Human Resources are called in after the fact and told to make the problem go away. In these institutions, the head of Human Resources is not a key player, and lacks the authority to hold bullies accountable. Targets and bystanders typically do not go to Human Resources because they know that they have no power and/or courage to properly intervene. People working in human resources in these cultures know what bullying is because they are bullied themselves and are cowed into thinking that this goes with the territory.

In Dictatorial cultures, Human Resources are also called in after the fact and told to make the problem go away. Here the head of Human Resources could be a key player and, if so, is part of the problem. Bullies in these cultures are considered heroes because they are viewed as high performers and have more credibility than their targets. Bullies know this and manipulate Human Resources to become their allies. Where legislation exists, policies and procedures are put into place but not into practice; compliance is for legal and security reasons versus prevention.

In many cases, heads of Human Resources have the technical and academic credentials to be the best and the brightest in the profession, but lack the influence and/or courage to prevent and stop bullying from occurring. As in Disjointed cultures, human resource people know what bullying is, because they are bullied and, because of the environment in which they work, they tend to become a bully who is targeted by another bully.

In Stable cultures, Human Resources are mandated to ensure employees are free and safe from bullying. Here, the head of Human Resources is a key player and has the authority, not only to hold bullies accountable, but more importantly, prevent bullying from occurring. Legislation does not drive policies and procedures being put in place. They have been in place and are firmly entrenched and integrated in the way business is conducted. Where there are incidents, Human Resources conducts a swift, but comprehensive, investigation and resolves the situation. Targets and bystanders go to Human Resources because they trust both the system and the individual, and they are viewed as being neutral. Heads of Human Resources in these cultures are the best and the brightest of their profession because they apply their technical and academic backgrounds and experience and view their role as custodians of a positive culture. Human resource people working in these cultures know what bullying is because they have studied the topic.

While the CEO should own and drive the culture of an organization, the head of Human Resources should be responsible and accountable for the integrity of the cultural health of the organization in the same way the CFO is responsible and accountable for the integrity of the financial systems and reporting.

The head of Human Resources is in the best position, regardless of the culture, to stop bullying from occurring. This should not be a matter of choice; it is a requirement of the job. If the head of Human Resources is not equipped or does not have the courage to make it stop, s/he is in the wrong position and, as such, is part of the problem.

The following outlines what Human Resources should do to ensure that the work environment is safe and free from bullying.

1. Conduct a comprehensive annual risk assessment.

2. Report findings and a plan of action to senior management and the Board of Directors for their endorsement and approval.

3. Develop and institutionalize policies, procedures and programs that address the issue of workplace violence.

4. Include workplace violence in the code of conduct.

5. As part of the hiring of, and promotion to, a management position, have a psychological assessment be a condition of acceptance. No exemptions.

6. Develop a "Terms of Engagement" agreement for all senior staff to sign.

7. Ensure that the performance management systems are clear, fair, reasonable, and not ambiguous or subjective, thereby, not giving a bully the opportunity to entrap a target.

8. Regularly train managers and supervisors on:
   - Performance management
   - Policies, procedures and programs
   - Identifying risk behaviors
   - How to recognize, respond to, report on and prevent bullying

9. Conduct an annual awareness program for all employees outlining their rights and responsibilities on workplace violence.

10. Develop an incident investigation protocol that is swift, fair, objective, comprehensive, and minimizes the risk of the target becoming the villain.

11. In the event the CEO is also the CBO (Chief Bullying Officer), coach and guide him/her on changing attitudes and behaviors. If this is unsuccessful, this must be reported to the Chair of the Board of Directors for intervention.

12. Leverage the power of Emotional Intelligence.

Heads of Human Resources should view being part of the solution as a real opportunity to gain influence and relevance. Key to becoming part of the solution is to be credible as an honest broker who acts in the best interests of all concerned.

The Red Flags

If bullying occurs, there are always indicators that it is happening. If people in human resources do not monitor these indicators, they are part of the problem.

The majority of bullying incidents are not reported by either the target or the bystanders, but that does not mean it is not going on. Usually bullying is talked about amongst employees and bullies build a reputation. If bullies are not confronted, they are, in essence, allowed to run loose.

Other than employees talking amongst themselves, there are a number of indicators that can identify and expose bullying and the bullies. Human Resources needs to follow up on any and every indicator. Where there is a bully running loose, there are almost always a number of telltale signs and, by tying together what may appear to be seemingly unrelated comments, events and situations, the story can typically be discovered.

The following outlines the telltale signs that a bully or a number of bullies are running loose:

- The "noise level" or comments that people are making, directly and indirectly. If there is a bully running loose, people will talk about it. Human Resources needs to have employees keep them in the loop. If the other indicators of bullying are there and the people in Human Resources are not hearing the "noise level," they are out of the loop.

- Anonymous letters from people who are aware of a situation, but are afraid to bring it forward.

- Calls to a whistleblower hot line. If there are none, or few calls, this is an indicator that there may be fear in reporting wrongdoing.

- Comments made by employees on social media, e.g., blogs. Don't try to stop the blogs or identify employees who post—stop the reasons employees feel it necessary to post.

- High turnover is an indicator that something is amiss. This, connected with other indicators, could expose bullying.

- Exit interviews. When people leave, they should be asked whether bullying was a factor in their departure. People may not be direct in their comments, not wanting to burn bridges, but will usually give comments like, "He could be difficult to work with, or demanding, but we just learned to live with it." When comments like these are made, the interviewer should probe and make the person comfortable giving specifics.

- Increase in the absentee rate.

- Increase in the number of people on stress leave.

- Difficulty in getting people to transfer into a particular department or division.

- Engagement survey data comparison by department.

- Written comments that are made in engagement surveys. A lack of, or few written comments are an indicator that there could be a fear factor in expressing viewpoints or concerns.

- Comments made by vendors, recruiters and other service providers. While these people are external to the organization, they are often bystanders and may hear and see more of what is going on in an organization than the organizational leaders or Human Resource. These people could also be a bully's target.

- In organizations with medical departments, regular and ongoing dialogue on levels of stress within the organization.

- Calls made to the EAP (Employee Assistance Program). The providers of these programs should be required to make Human Resources aware of bullying, with the assurance that the target's confidentiality is protected. (In cultures of fear, EAPs may not be utilized because employees do not trust the system. Therefore, a decrease in calls, or a lower rate of calls than EAP providers' benchmark, is an indicator.)

- Inconsistencies in representations made by a manager to discipline or terminate a subordinate. (Review the subordinate's performance history compared to what the manager is claiming.)

- Managers who take all the credit when things go well and blame others when things go wrong.

- Individuals who constantly have disputes with others and are unwilling to compromise on their positions.

- Previous accusations or incidences of bullying.

On becoming aware of a situation or the probability of bullying occurring, the onus should be on Human Resources to check into it immediately.

The first step is to review all indicators that are available that would add credence or discount the allegation or the probability of bullying. This is where it is important to tie the seemingly unrelated comments, events and situations together. As much of this information should be readily available, it should not take an inordinate amount of time to pull together. Depending on the situation, it may be necessary to conduct interviews with people who are close to the situation.

Armed with this information, the Human Resource person should meet with the suspected bully's immediate supervisor to review the situation and determine who should meet with the suspected bully.

The purpose of the meeting is to indicate that bullying is suspected, along with the reasons. If there is not a specific complaint and there is no direct evidence, the person should not be accused of being a bully. However, it is appropriate to point out that there are indicators that bullying is occurring and the organization is obliged to investigate and take the necessary steps to make sure that it isn't.

It is also appropriate to challenge the person on the reasons the indicators are there, for example, asking why turnover is high. The ideal outcome is to have the person acknowledge that there is validity to the concerns being raised and agree to change the behavior. If this happens, the person should be asked what the organization can do to help change the behavior, for example, help with anger management. It should be clear that the expectation is the indicators will change; for example, decreased turnover and a much lower "noise level."

In situations where the person denies being a bully and rationalizes the indicators, then a more comprehensive investigation should be conducted. The person who is suspected of being a bully should be made aware of this and informed that people who are close to the investigation will be interviewed. It should also be made very clear that any intimidation or retaliation against people being interviewed will result in severe disciplinary action, up to, and including, discharge.

The investigation should be swift, objective and comprehensive.

If, in the investigation, bullying is validated, the bully must be dealt with. Part of the investigation should be an assessment as to whether the bully can be rehabilitated.

If the assessment concludes that the bully cannot change, the bully must be removed from the situation. If s/he is moved within the organization, it is important that this move is not seen as a reward.

If the assessment concludes that the bully can change, the organization should offer to put a corrective action plan in place and closely monitor the situation.

CASE STUDY

Onto Pleasure Island—Pam's story

In 2007, an executive recruiter approached Pam about an opportunity to join a global pharmaceutical company. Pam regarded the executive recruiter as a friend as they had worked for the same company a number of years earlier. The recruiter's commendation that this opportunity would be a good fit for Pam was the sole reason she considered the job.

At the time, Pam was a highly successful executive for another pharmaceutical company. In the ten years she worked for the company, she had been promoted six times. Prior to this, Pam spent six years as a top performer in the packaged goods industry after graduating from university.

After the initial meeting with the executive recruiter, Pam met with the company's CEO Karl on a number of occasions and Ellen the EVP of Human Resources. Pam had some reservations about taking the position, as she had heard from people who she trusted that the CEO was difficult to work for. Some even described him as a bully. Pam talked to the executive recruiter who assured her the rumors were not true.

Both the executive recruiter and Ellen assured Pam that, while Karl was very direct, he was a fantastic leader, a visionary, very ethical, and fostered a real team spirit.

Had Pam done more research before accepting the position, she would have learned that Karl was, in addition to being the CEO, he was also the CBO (Chief Bullying Officer), and that the company had many of the characteristics of what I refer to as a "Dictatorial" culture. Pam's story highlights the importance of doing due diligence before deciding to change organizations.

Karl and Ellen were very aggressive in their pursuit of Pam. Karl, Pam later learned, had been overheard saying that he "nabbed a trophy hire" from a competitor.

Pam was offered a compensation package significantly higher than what she was making and a guarantee of a promotion within the first year. These were clear indicators that she was a strategic hire and would be a contender to become Karl's replacement.

Based on what Pam felt was "a deal simply too good to pass up," she accepted the offer.

When Pam joined the company, her first priority was to meet with all the managers in her department. In these meetings, most of the managers indicated that there were major cultural issues in the department and that the issues were linked to Nicole, one of Pam's direct reports. There were accusations that Nicole bullied people, within the department and throughout the organization. The Human Resource representative for the department provided background on Nicole and data that showed turnover in the department was high, largely due to Nicole's bullying. There was also an independent mediator's report, which likened Nicole's leadership within the department to the movies *Mean Girls* and *Lord of the Flies*. Others in the company spoke about a long history of Nicole being constantly combative and pitting her team against others in the company. For some reason, she seemed to have been able to do this with impunity.

Almost from the beginning, Pam found that Nicole was undermining her and treated her as if she had no authority. Nicole routinely refused to communicate directly with her, publicly refused to attend key meetings and walked out on meetings. Pam also became aware that Nicole and Karl met on a regular basis without informing her. Nicole made it clear to Pam that she felt that she was more qualified than Pam to run the department.

In meetings with her peers, Pam learned that there was a lot of speculation that Karl and Nicole were having an affair, which was commonly known within the company and across the industry. The speculation gained some credibility with Pam when she, Karl and Nicole went on a field trip. Pam drove and Karl and Nicole ignored her the entire day. At the end of the day, Karl and Nicole went out for dinner without inviting Pam.

Pam went to Ellen for advice. Ellen went to great lengths to assure Pam that there was no merit to the speculation; that she had spoken to Karl about it, and he acknowledged that he and Nicole had a strong working relationship, but it did not go beyond that. Ellen's advice was for Pam to meet with Nicole and confront her on the behavioral issues.

Pam met with Nicole, who reacted badly and insisted that a meeting be held with her, Karl, Ellen and Pam. Pam agreed with this and they met the next day.

At this meeting, Karl and Ellen clearly wanted to appease Nicole, complimenting her on her performance and suggesting that her passion and dedication caused her to behave the way she did. Nicole agreed that this was the case, but claimed she did not mean to offend anyone and that, while she was disappointed in not getting Pam's position, she wanted to support her nonetheless.

Pam wanted to reach an understanding that, if Nicole were going to meet with the CEO, Pam be made aware of it, and that the CEO would not make decisions based on one-sided information. This was agreed to. But Pam didn't feel relieved. She walked away from the meeting with her worst fears confirmed. Ellen and Karl were trying to pacify Nicole and Pam. Nothing changed. Nicole continued to walk out of meetings with Pam, sent her out-dated marketing reports to present at meetings, bullied Pam's employees and had private meetings with Karl.

Almost immediately after the meeting, Karl started going after Pam with a litany of tactics designed to set her up for failure, including suggesting that Pam was leaking internal information to a competitor (which is what Karl did with a number of people he targeted, as a way to get them out). Other tactics included leaving her out of key communications, making decisions in her area without informing her, leaving her out of key reports and emails to the management committee and continuing to deal directly with Nicole.

Pam now had no doubt that she was in trouble, but had no idea what to do. It seemed like a bad dream. Her life and career had been so on track just six months earlier. In the wonderful Pinocchio story, remember Honest John and Gideon easily tempting the children away from school and onto Pleasure Island with promises of untold amusement and treats, but not a hint of what happened to the children there? Pam could relate.

Pam went to a number of peers for advice. While all of them were sympathetic, none wanted to get involved because they were afraid of Karl and none of them trusted Ellen. Pam learned that earlier in the year, five people went to the Board of Directors expressing ethical concerns they had about Karl, including their speculation about his affair with Nicole.

The situation was taking a serious toll on Pam's health. She was unable to sleep and began losing weight. The situation was so unreal and unjust that she constantly wondered if she had done something to deserve this. Within the company, Pam had no one to confide in. Her relationships with friends and family became increasingly strained. Pam finally sought professional help and was diagnosed with Post Traumatic Stress Disorder.

Pam then went for legal advice. The lawyer advised her to file for constructive dismissal, which she did, and negotiate a severance package. She left the company a broken woman with no allies, including the executive recruiter, who she firmly believes knew what Karl was like. The executive recruiter stopped returning her calls.

The story does not end here. A few months later, Pam landed another position. She received a glowing six-month review with a comment on how well she fit into the workplace culture. A couple of weeks after the review, her new CEO requested an introduction to Karl so that he could make a sales pitch. Pam facilitated the introduction. Less than twenty-four hours after facilitating the introduction, the CEO fired Pam, saying she was a "poor fit." There was no question in Pam's mind that Karl had discredited her to the CEO and Karl made doing business with them conditional on Pam being fired.

Fortunately, because Pam was highly regarded in the industry and had a solid track record prior to going to "Pleasure Island," she was able to relocate and is gainfully employed with an organization whose values are more in line with hers. While this is a happy ending for Pam, it is unlikely that she will ever fully recover from the horrible experience and will always have to be concerned that Karl will seek further retaliation.

The Board of Directors did confront Karl on the issues brought forward by the five "whistleblowers" and conducted a cursory investigation (they did not even interview three individuals suggested by the whistleblowers who could provide specific details on the allegations made). They claim not to have found any wrongdoing. Karl adamantly denied the affair. Even after Karl was caught by a private investigator leaving Nicole's home after spending the night there and the evidence was given to the board, they still did nothing. This was in and around the same time that the Hewlett Packard board fired its CEO because of circumstances around an affair he was alleged to have had with a contract employee.

As time went on, Karl became even bolder in his questionable business practices and in his relationship with Nicole—he was, some suspected, taunting the board into firing him to trigger his "golden parachute."

Four of the five whistleblowers were forced out of the company and discovered that they were under surveillance. Phones and emails were monitored before and after they left, and company funds were used for this activity. These people also found that they were blacklisted.

Thirteen months after the "cursory" investigation, a key group of employees staged a revolt and Karl abruptly resigned.

AUTHOR'S NOTE—This case study captures the profile of a CBO, illustrates Human Resources' culpability and highlights the board's negligence.

Over the course of my career, I have dealt with a large number of boss/subordinate affairs that created problems in the organization. One, in particular, stands out when a board member challenged me by stating, "This is commonplace. It's part of human nature." I expressed that I was offended that he thought I was that naive and questioned,

1. "Is it okay for the CEO to breach company policy?"

2. "If he is breaching this policy, is it possible he is breaching other policies?"

3. "If the CEO is exempt from certain policies, how can they be enforced with others?"

4. "Is it okay for the subordinate to receive extreme favoritism because of the relationship?"

5. "Is it okay for the subordinate to abuse her power and bully others because of her access to the CEO?"

6. "Is it okay that the majority of management lost respect and confidence in the CEO?"

I indicated that, as in most cases of this nature, "The affair is a secondary issue. It is what happens because of the affair that is harmful."

Even with my retort, I don't think the board member got it!

CASE STUDY

Alone in a man's world—Sonya's story

After graduating from university in 2004, Sonya enrolled in an elite firefighting academy and completed six months of rigorous training. Sonya was the only female in a class of thirty.

After graduating from the academy, Sonya joined a fire department in a mid-sized municipality. As in the academy, Sonya was the only female on the force. Initially, the relationship with her captain and fellow firefighters was positive.

By the time Sonya had two years in, she had come to know Rob, her captain, quite well. Sonya was twenty-eight years old at the time and the Captain was fifty-seven. As a firefighter, it is key to be a team player, and because you are working in close proximity for long periods of time, developing close bonds is critical.

Sonya felt comfortable with Rob and viewed him, not only as her superior, but also a mentor. Sonya knew that Rob had taken her under his wing and thought that his interest in her was strictly professional.

Over time, Rob's attentions started to cross the line. He was giving Sonya a lot of special attention, singling her out for preferred assignments, always trying to sit next to her during meals, calling her on the intercom letting her know he was going to bed, etc. The other firefighters started to notice what was going on and Rob's actions became the fodder for gossip and jokes.

While Rob's attentions were never overt or threatening, they were starting to make Sonya very uncomfortable. There was no question in Sonya's mind that Rob had a crush on her.

Sonya contemplated going to Rob and telling him his attentions were making her uncomfortable. However, she decided against this because she observed that Rob had a mean streak and retaliated against those who crossed him.

Sonya decided that her best option was to request a transfer to another station. Although she did not file a formal complaint, Sonya did tell the Senior Captain the reason for her request. An immediate transfer was arranged.

A few weeks after the transfer, Sonya ran into Rob when they were both off duty. Sonya was friendly, but distant. Rob called her at home that night and demanded to know why she requested the transfer and why she was so distant with him. Sonya indicated that his call was totally inappropriate and he hung up on her.

The next time Sonya was scheduled to be on duty, she was told that Rob was in the captain's office and wanted to meet with her. Sonya was frightened and refused to meet with him. While Sonya hid upstairs, she overheard Rob go into a tirade with her captain.

From that point, Rob mounted a campaign against Sonya. He was furious that she was rejecting and avoiding him.

Although they worked at different locations, and she worked for a different captain, Rob still exercised considerable influence over her. In situations where all stations were called into an emergency (which is often the case), Sonya was under his command.

Rob initiated a letter-writing campaign. He coerced firefighters to write the Senior Captain with fictitious concerns about Sonya's judgment and physical fitness, and that they considered her a safety risk. In addition to sending these "reports" to the Senior Captain, photocopies were widely circulated. When off duty, Rob constantly worked the phones encouraging his cronies to find any reason to "write her up."

On a number of occasions, she witnessed Rob speaking with her fellow firefighters, pointing in her direction, and walking away shaking his head.

The campaign worked. Sonya was shunned by her fellow firefighters. They whispered amongst themselves, gave her sideways looks, and head shaking was routine. Few spoke to her and she was excluded from most activities at the station, alone in a man's world!

Sonya also found that her equipment and gear were tampered with. On one occasion, all of her gear and nametag were removed. When she found her overhead bag, she found her nametag along with an open box cutter. Had Sonya just reached into her bag she could have seriously cut herself. Fortunately, she was not hurt, but her sense of security was badly shaken. When Sonya reported this to her captain, he accused her of deflecting the concerns he and her fellow firefighters had regarding her being a safety risk.

Sonya then felt that, not only was her job at risk, but also her personal safety. This was reinforced when she ran into Rob at her station and he threatened that something bad would happen if she stayed and that, by staying, she was putting everyone she worked with at risk.

This was the breaking point for Sonya and, in November of 2007, she formally complained on the advice of a lawyer friend.

Initially, the complaint was filed with the Senior Captain, who referred it to an Assistant Deputy Chief who dealt with workplace harassment, discrimination and abuse issues. The advisor wrote up a report that went directly to the Chief who immediately forwarded it to the city's director of Human Resources who initiated an investigation.

It was clear to Sonya at the outset that this was the first time anything like this had occurred in the municipality. The union representing the firefighters initially resisted the investigation and needed to be educated on the legalities involved as well as the process. This resulted in a delayed investigation.

Almost everyone in the squad was interviewed. Most were clearly uncomfortable with it and made it known to Sonya that they did not like it. The fear factor was also at play and they knew that if it got back to Rob that they supported Sonya's claim, Rob was capable of retaliation. Sonya's isolation got worse; they resented a female junior firefighter taking on a very senior captain. Fortunately, there were a few who supported Sonya's position, particularly those who had their own experiences with Rob.

Confidentiality became an issue, and it was obvious to Sonya that there was a lot of talk going on. After people were interviewed, they huddled amongst themselves to compare notes.

Sonya was interviewed a number of times during the process and often felt that she was fighting this alone against Rob, her coworkers, the union and, to some extent, the administration.

During the interviews, the investigator challenged whether Sonya was able to do the work of a firefighter. The director of Human Resources offered to move her to another department. Through all of this, Sonya remained resolved.

The investigation took a long 379 days, over a year, to complete. During this period, the isolation, fear and anxiety affected her health, requiring her to call in sick thirteen times. Sonya knew when she would not be able to perform as a firefighter, and if there were a fire when she felt this way, she would be a safety risk.

Finally, the Investigator completed his report and found that her complaint had merit and the treatment she received was unjust. Included in the report were references to other situations where Rob bullied his subordinates.

By mutual agreement, Rob took early retirement.

Following the investigator's recommendations, all departments in the city conducted a cultural assessment and a number of positive changes were made to ensure that employees were not at risk of being bullied. Everyone went through an extensive awareness program on bullying and everyone in a supervisory position went through an extensive training program on bullying. The city is now considered a model for good leadership and staff relations. Also, there is a much more streamlined process to investigate complaints.

Sonya credits the director of Human Resources for helping her cope through this long ordeal and keeping in touch with her to see how she was doing and also to assure her that the investigation was not forgotten. While the director of Human Resources should be credited for doing the right thing, the investigation took far too long. Sonya went through sheer hell for several years—the length of time it took to conduct the investigation!

AUTHOR'S NOTE—As indicated in the study, although the municipality and the director of Human Resources did the right things, next to the bullying, the big issue here is the bureaucratic culture where an already bad situation was worsened by the time it took to resolve. This is often the case in situations I've been brought into. Bullying must be investigated promptly. Many human resource professionals become slaves to the bureaucracy, and process becomes a substitute for purpose.

Conducting a Workplace Assessment: Determining "At Risk" Position

The 2012 collapse of the 168-year-old *News of the World* and the public humiliation of media mogul Rupert Murdoch should cause organizational leaders to satisfy themselves that their cultures do not put their organizations at risk.

Murdoch's testimony before the British Parliamentary Committee was, in essence, an admission that he was totally out of the loop of how his organizations operate. His reputation as a hands-on manager makes his defense questionable. While we suspect that Murdoch may have been aware of some of the tactics used to get the scoops scored by his newspapers, it is entirely possible that he did not fully understand or appreciate how a culture of fear can destroy an organization and people. While Murdoch places the blame on those he trusted, he and his board should, at the very least, acknowledge management neglect.

Many organizational leaders relegate the "cultural stuff" to their human resource people, believing that it is sufficient to have values and operating principles plastered all over the place, rarely assessing whether they are consistently applied and are reflected in the actual culture that exists.

I have found that it usually takes a major incident for organizational leaders to consider bullying a major risk. In all of the instances where I was called in, leaders in the organization were shocked to find that the incident could have been prevented had they paid closer attention to telltale signs. They were also amazed at how little they really knew about what was going on in their organizations.

A comprehensive review of a number of fronts is necessary to determine the actual culture that exists within an organization. As all of the areas are related, reviewing and analyzing them in isolation will not reveal the whole picture. Connecting this analysis with cultural indicators yields insights that should capture the attention of even the most hardened and skeptical leader.

When I conduct assessments for organizations, I go below the surface, helping organizational leaders gain information that may not be obvious or not brought to their attention. I look for undisclosed workplace cultural issues and connect seemingly unrelated comments, events and situations to identify the risks and opportunities.

The assessment process has four stages that are customized based on individual organizational needs.

The four stages are as follows:

Stage 1: Documentation and Program Review

I review and assess the effectiveness of the organization's:

- Policies and procedures

- Definition of workplace bullying and violence

- Employee surveys and their robustness

- Employee complaints

- Past incidence reports

- Employment programs
- Incident investigations

Stage 2: Analyze the Fronts

This stage involves gaining a comprehensive interview-based understanding of the workplace. Employees at various levels are interviewed with assurances of confidentiality to determine workplace dynamics and the strengths and weaknesses of the organizational structure. This is where I delve into the eleven fronts:

1. Governance
2. Structure
3. Decision-making
4. Politics
5. Systems and technology
6. Communication
7. Roles and responsibilities
8. Accountabilities
9. Measurements
10. Rewards and recognition
11. Alignment

Stage 3: Review Cultural Indicators

A review and analysis of a number of cultural indicators will help identify the effect that culture has on the individual and the organization. The indicators are:

- Staff turnover—overall organization—by department—by employee category.

- Run rate vacancies by department—by employee category.

- Absentee rate, short and long term—by department—by employee category.

- Stress-leave experience.

- Frequency and severity of workplace accidents.

- History of suicides or attempted suicides.

- Participation rate of people using an employee assistance program (EAP).

- Proportion of internal promotions to external hires for positions beyond entry level.

- Termination rate (i.e., those who are fired)—overall organization—by department.

- Resignation rate—overall organization—by department.

- Reasons people cite for leaving.

- History of grievances or complaints.

- History of human rights claims filed.

- Activity on whistleblower hot line or other vehicles used to report wrongdoings.

Stage 4: Report and Recommendations

In the final stage, I present the outcome of the assessment process:

- Identification of risk behaviors in the organization.

- A fear-factor gauge.

- Report on the effect of existing systems, processes and practices.

- Recommendations for creating a sustainable, integrated anti-bullying program.

- Baseline from which to annually measure improvement.

Benefits of conducting a comprehensive workplace assessment:

1. Provides senior management with the organization's risk profile.

2. Determines the prevalence of incidents and a baseline from which to track trending of risk profile.

3. Identifies areas of highest risk within the overall organization, which assists in prioritizing changes and interventions.

4. Satisfies legislative compliance requirements.

5. Provides a unique insight in what is really going on in an organization.

Whether an organization resembles a large public enterprise such as Murdoch's *News of the World* or a small, privately run manufacturing or consulting concern, its leaders require an appreciation of the risks created from workplace culture. The damages arising to individuals, the brand, and, indeed, the enterprise, from a culture of intimidation, fear and bullying, is as significant to an organization's well-being as those risks reviewed regularly by corporate accountants, lawyers and risk managers. I believe that any Board of Directors and/or executive management team will benefit enormously from the heightened cultural awareness this assessment process reveals. Where an organization's culture and operational systems are positive, transparent and predictable, its employees, customers and shareholders will reward it with positive activities of their own.

Unions and Bullying

In 1972, I began my career as a management labor relations officer in a Chrysler plant in Windsor, Ontario. There, I learned—by total immersion—conflict management. Mildly put, the environment was toxic and barbarically tribal. Most of my time and energy was spent preventing fistfights between workers and foremen (pretty scary for a 140 lb., 23-year-old) and encouraging everyone in the plant, from the supervisor to the janitor, to be more delicate in their language.

My experience with unions also includes a ten-year stint as chief spokesman for Loblaw, Canada's largest retail food chain—which, at the time, was 90 percent unionized.

A few decades ago, unions were necessary to protect the rights and represent the interests of workers. It is safe to say that, with recent economic downturns, all too many employees have been, and are, exploited. Given this, it is perplexing that, during this period, union membership in the private sector has, and continues to, decline.

The reasons for the decline can easily be rationalized by blaming Right to Work Legislation in some states. In many cases, management responds to organizing drives by bullying employees with the threat of closing or moving their operations offshore and targeting employees who are considered ring leaders.

In situations where I have been brought in to consult with management on organizing drives, most executives' first instinct is to kill the drive at any cost. When I question why their employees feel it necessary to be represented, the reaction is usually hostile silence.

There is no question that legislation and the fear factor are valid explanations for the decline of unionized labor.

Valid as they may be, there is a much bigger factor at play—that is how unions are viewed by workers. The prevailing view among union workers is that unions bully their members into doing (or not doing) things that conflict with their interests, values and beliefs.

For example, in Ontario, Canada, in 2013, teachers were bullied into withdrawing from extracurricular activities to protest their legislated inability to strike—withdrawal of the extracurricular activities was a form of "work to rule."

A large contingent of teachers did not support this action because it went against their professional philosophy. Notwithstanding their objections, most complied with the "work to rule" out of fear. It takes courage to go against the union because those who do will likely be viewed as traitors by the die-hards and union leaders.

Unions have evolved to become social activists and a major lobbying force, which, in many cases, is for admirable causes. Some of this activism, however, is in conflict with the interests, values and beliefs of their members. Union leaders have not responded well to the changing diversity of the membership and are still far too rigid in the notion that "if you are a brother or sister—there is solidarity."

Solidarity is important for any association or organization; however, when it becomes absolute and enforced through bullying, it is no different than what I describe as a Dictatorial culture.

In some cases, the issues loom even larger. In late 2014 and early 2015, the New York Police Department instituted a work slowdown, ostensibly in response to a perceived lack of support from Mayor Bill DeBlasio. Criminal summonses and traffic tickets were down more than 90 percent from the previous year. Apart from the financial repercussions for the city—it was estimated the stoppage cost New York $10 million each week in paid fines—there is the even more serious issue of civic safety.

A dysfunctional police department has consequences that reach far beyond police station walls, putting New Yorkers at risk. The unions claimed they weren't behind the work stoppage, but the work stoppage ended as quickly, universally and quietly as it began once the Police Commissioner announced that it would. Workplace culture and the role unions play has ramifications throughout the organization and every single person and institution it touches.

CASE STUDY

Who does my union represent?— Patrick's story

Patrick was a city planner for a large North American city. He was one of 26 planners, and they were represented by a union for municipal employees. Discharged in 2010, Patrick had been with the city for fifteen years.

In July of 2009, the city approached the union for concessions to help reduce a major deficit. The union held a member meeting to review this. At the meeting, Patrick indicated that the planning department was operating well under their capacity. This is something that Patrick had brought forward to his manager on a number of occasions, usually when a planner left and they were recruiting for a replacement. Patrick's view was that he and the other planners could process double what they were doing. Every time he raised this with his manager, Patrick was told that the workload was negotiated with the union and to change this would be impossible.

After the meeting, Doug, the union representative, responded, "Are you crazy? Never, and I repeat, never raise this again!" Patrick fought back by pointing out the city was in trouble and needed to find ways to reduce costs and, as a loyal employee, he felt obligated to express his views.

"In fact," he added, "I know in speaking with people in most departments, there are the same opportunities to reduce costs throughout the organization." Doug told Patrick it was not his place to offer solutions.

Patrick was disturbed and decided to prove his point. Starting immediately, he processed the daily assignments by noon and requested additional assignments. Patrick's manager refused to do this because it would be in violation of the collective agreement.

Not satisfied, Patrick went to the director of Human Resources and was told the same thing, and was advised to "just leave it alone." Prior to this meeting, Patrick reviewed the collective agreement and could find no reference to workload. When he challenged the director on this, she indicated that it was an "unwritten understanding."

For two months, Patrick finished his assignments by noon, without exerting himself. During this period, he consistently had his manager review his work to ensure quality was not compromised. The manager indicated that she was satisfied with the quality of work.

A coworker told Doug, the union representative, of Patrick's actions. Doug called Patrick and warned him that if he did not stop, his job would be at risk. Patrick responded that he wasn't doing anything wrong; in fact, what he was doing was the right thing to do to help the city improve their finances. Patrick also argued that it was the union's responsibility to find ways to help the city, thereby, protecting jobs.

Almost every day after this, Patrick received anonymous threatening emails and calls to his home. The response from the director of Human Resources to his complaint was,

"I warned you; you brought this on yourself and there is nothing we can do to help you."

Concurrent with the threatening emails and calls, Patrick's manager started to write Patrick up for poor quality work. At a disciplinary meeting, Patrick produced a record of the times he asked his manager to assess the quality of the work and each time he received a positive review. The manager indicated she took a closer look at the work. Doug also attended the meeting and advised Patrick that he had to support the manager and, if the quality of work did not improve, the union would not be able to protect him. Patrick requested that an independent third party be brought in to assess his work. The request was denied. Patrick also requested that an investigation be done on the threatening emails and calls. This request was also denied and he was accused of being the instigator of the emails and calls.

Not one to give up, Patrick went to the police to report the emails and calls. An investigation was conducted. Doug and Patrick's coworkers were questioned. The investigation was inconclusive and Patrick was told that the only thing the police could do was keep the file on record. The emails, calls and poor reviews continued for the next few months.

In January of 2010, Patrick was fired for poor performance, and his salary and benefits were immediately terminated. The union did not file a grievance.

In March, Patrick suffered a major heart attack and had a triple bypass. After recovering, he is legally challenging the union for failing to represent him and is filing a civil wrongful dismissal case against the city.

Part Two:

The Dynamics of Bullying

"There is exploitation when the Master considers
the Worker not as an associate, as a helper, but as
an instrument from which he must draw the
greatest service at the lowest possible cost.
The exploitation of man by man is slavery."
—FREDERIC OZANAM

What Exactly Is Bullying?

In the work that I have done on bullying in the workplace and the interviews conducted during the course of writing this book, I am amazed at the lack of understanding and awareness on the topic, as well as the myths and misinterpretations out there.

The Dignity at Work Campaign in the United Kingdom defines workplace bullying as, "Persistent, offensive, abusive, intimidating, malicious or insulting behavior, abuse of power or unfair penal sanctions, which makes the recipient feel upset, threatened, humiliated or vulnerable, which undermines their self confidence and which may cause them to suffer stress."

Profile of a Bully

As we witnessed with the Lance Armstrong debacle, bullying is all about power, control, deceit, deflection discrediting, destruction and denial.

For over a decade, Armstrong was considered "The Boss" of the ICU—"The International Cycling Union"—and he had total control over the doping culture of the U.S. (Postal Service) team. In essence, he was the Chief Bullying Officer of the sport.

Armstrong bullied to:

- force teammates to use banned substances

- retaliate against those who took an anti-doping stance

- force off of the team those who did not comply

- force off of the team those who testified against him

- discredit those who went against him

- keep people in the know from exposing him

- influence the ICU

In a *60 Minutes* interview, Scott Pelley asked the U.S. Anti-doping Agency (USADA) CEO Travis Tygart what Armstrong could do to those who testified against him. Tygart's response was that Armstrong would "Incinerate" anyone who went against him. Tygart himself was bullied and received an anonymous death threat during the course of the investigation he conducted.

Armstrong's behaviors, demeanor and comments exposed him as a classic narcissistic bully. The Diagnostic and Statistical Manual of Mental Disorders IV classifies those who have a narcissistic disorder as "those who:

- are preoccupied with fantasies of unlimited success;

- believe that they are special and unique;

- require excessive admiration;

- possess a strong sense of entitlement;

- exploit others and lack empathy;

- exhibit high levels of arrogance."

My experience in dealing with bullies—particularly those with power and control—is that they generally exhibit these narcissistic characteristics. Many are psychopaths and it may well be determined that Armstrong is one (see "Is There a Psychopath in the House?"). People with this disorder are dangerous and responsible for much of the violence in the workplace.

Bullying in the workplace is violence in the workplace. Most organizational leaders have difficulty identifying it in those terms, which I assert is the major reason that bullying is condoned and, in many situations, encouraged and, in many organizations, even expected.

The Dynamics of Bullying

David Beale and Helge Hoel in "Workplace Bullying: Industrial Relations and the Challenge for Management in Britain and Sweden," (*Industrial Relations and Management*; 2011 edition) reported that, "Very often, in 70 to 80 percent of the cases, the main culprit occupies a supervisory role while the target is a subordinate."

This is consistent with research done in North America. Coworkers also bully, but they are usually bystanders who, in many instances, become complicit in the bullying.

The Dignity at Work Campaign in the U.K. offers the following as some of the common ways that bullies torment their targets.

"Bullies may:

- Use terror tactics, open aggression, threats, shouting, abuse and obscenities toward their target.

- Subject their target to constant humiliation or ridicule, belittling their efforts, often in front of others.

- Subject their target to excessive supervision, monitoring everything they do and being excessively critical of minor things.

- Take credit for other people's work, but never take the blame when things go wrong.

- Override the person's authority.

- Remove significant work responsibilities from the person, reducing their job to routine tasks that are well below their skills and capabilities.

- Set impossible objectives or constantly change work requirements without notice, and then criticize or reprimand the person for not meeting demands.

- Ostracize and marginalize their target, working through third parties, excluding the person from discussions, decisions, etc.

- Spread malicious rumors about the individual.

- Refuse reasonable requests for leave, training etc., or block promotions."

Based on the many cases I have worked on, the following also could apply:

- Unreasonably delaying approvals, or rejecting plans or objectives.

- Not providing constructive feedback.

- Making negative comments about the target to others.

- Dealing directly with the target's subordinates and ordering the subordinate not to disclose this.

The Five Forms of Bullying

There are five kinds of bullying: verbal, psychological, physical, cyber and blacklisting. Schoolyard bullying by children and pre-adults is far more overt, whereas, bullying in the workplace is far more calculated.

Most often, in the workplace, a combination of verbal, psychological and cyber bullying is applied—whereas, in schools, it is more of a combination of verbal, cyber and physical, or the threat of physical violence.

In schools, bullies use cyber bullying to discredit, embarrass or "out" their targets. The same applies to the workplace; however, it is more extensively used by the bully boss who does it under the guise of performance management.

My direct experience with being targeted was after I exposed a corrupt executive. For well over a year, I was subject to a combination of psychological, cyber and, (if you include a death threat as physical bullying), physical, bullying in retaliation for blowing the whistle. My phones were tapped, my emails were hacked, I was called a "f—ing faggot" in a public forum and, for a period of time, put under surveillance. When I reported this, the Board of Directors chose to believe the executive, and only when I produced documented evidence, did they start to believe me.

1. Verbal bullying

> "People who are brutally honest get more
> satisfaction out of the brutality than the honesty."
> —RICHARD J. NEEDHAM

It is very easy for a bully, especially on a one-on-one basis, to verbally abuse a target, which makes it the most common form of bullying. The bully usually rationalizes or defends the behaviors as "just kidding," or "I did not mean to offend, it is just my style," or "I lash out because of my passion," or "it's my way of getting people to produce more."

2. Psychological bullying

"Calumny requires no proof. The throwing out of malicious imputations against any character leaves a stain which no after-refutation can wipe out. To create an unfavourable impression, it is not necessary that certain things should be true, but that they have been said."
–WILLIAM HAZLITT

Bullies are masters of deflection and manipulation who usually set their targets up to emotionally destroy them, which they know will have an effect on the target's performance, attendance and attitude, which, in turn, gives the bully the ammunition to get rid of the target.

Psychological bullying is the most difficult form of bullying to deal with. It is usually not just one comment, situation or event, it is a combination of things, well-thought-out by the bully. When things start seeming out of the norm, it is important to tie seemingly unrelated comments, events and situations together.

3. Physical bullying

"Violence is, essentially, a confession of
ultimate inarticulateness."
–*TIME* MAGAZINE

Physical violence is more common in the schoolyard than in the workplace. However, when you consider the threat of physical violence as well as actual violence, it becomes more common.

A September 2012 *Forbes* article by Meghan Casserly called "When Snitches Get Stitches: Physical Violence as Workplace Retaliation on the Rise" reported that "The number one weapon used at work is the fist" according to Larry Barton, a former professor at Harvard Business School and a leading expert on workplace violence. Barton estimates that more than 1.2 million Americans were physically assaulted in 2011.

According to the American Nurses Association, "The health-care sector leads all other industries, with 45 percent of all non-fatal attacks against workers resulting in lost work days in the US" (BLC, 2006).

Hazing is also a form of physical bullying that does not receive the exposure it should. Targets are usually new hires or workers regarded as different in some way. Being a target of aggression is perhaps the most humiliating experience that one can face in the workplace and, in all too many environments, it is considered harmless fun.

4. Cyber bullying

In today's world, cyber bullying has grown to the extent that it is now considered a major category of bullying. I assert that most bullies are cowards and technology has given too many the opportunity to be brave. According to the United States National Crime Prevention Council, cyber bullying occurs "when the Internet, cell phones or other devices are used to send or post texts or images intended to hurt or embarrass another person."

Bully managers use email to harass their targets and ratio-nalize it as an effective form of performance management. One individual I interviewed received emails from her boss every day including weekends and holidays, at all hours, day and night, for over two years which, in each instance, demanded an immediate response. In many cases, the intent of the emails from bullies is to provoke an angry response from the target. Chat rooms and anonymous emails are increasingly used to gossip about, and discredit, targets.

5. Blacklisting

In many instances, the bullying does not stop after the target leaves the situation. It is a small world and, when the target is in the bully's trap, the bully continues to discredit the target. In the interviews I conducted, many had great difficulty getting re-established, like Vera in "Vera's Story." I am astonished by the naivety of the so-called professionals who advise people who are targeted to quit, not realizing that the bully usually follows the target, making it almost impossible to get out of the trap.

The Dynamics of Bullying
at Play

As you have seen in Vera's story, and will see in the other stories, bullies are masters of deflection who usually discredit
their targets until the target also becomes the villain—they usually "kiss up and kick down" (as Stanford Engineering School
Management Professor Robert Sutton, author of, *Good Boss,
Bad Boss,* labeled it). Because they are seen as high producers,
they are viewed as heroes who garner more credibility than the
target.

Part One deals with the organizational dynamics of bullying
and, as you will see in the case studies, the following organizational characteristics are at play:

- A Dictatorial or a Disjointed culture

- A culture that rewards the bully and blames the target

- Practices that encourage individualism more than team

- A culture where power is vested without checks and
  balances.

Also in the stories, you will see a pattern that is usually evident in bullying:

- A triggering event that the bully takes exception to, which is usually a comment, criticism, challenge or action. The trigger frequently occurs when the bully views the target as a threat.

- The bully resolves to punish the target.

- The bully, bullies.

- The bystanders become complicit.

- The target falls into the bully's trap.

- If caught, the bullies deflect by turning the target into the culprit.

- The target is reprimanded, gets fired or quits.

- The bully identifies the next target.

- In all too few instances, bystanders become witnesses and defenders.

- In even rarer instances, the targets take steps to challenge the bully.

- The target finds it difficult to find alternative employment even after s/he leaves the toxic situation.

Making Distinctions

"A point of view can be a dangerous luxury when
substituted for insight and understanding."
–MARSHALL MCLUHAN, THE GUTENBERG GALAXY

Much of this book describes and illustrates what bullying is. One of the most frequent push-backs I get, particularly from people who are in management, is the fear that by raising the awareness of bullying, employees will use it as a shield or a sword and that it will restrict managers from being able to do their jobs out of fear they will be labeled as a bully. It is, therefore, necessary to be clear and make distinctions about what does and what does not constitute bullying.

Disagreements and conflict are a normal dynamic that occur in all environments. It would be wrong to label all disagreements and conflicts as bullying. It is healthy to raise and debate differing views, as long as it is done in an open, honest, and direct way, and resolved—even if the resolution is to "agree to disagree." Not only is it healthy to have these debates, I assert it is essential to bring differences out in the open, rather than have them fester.

As I discussed in "Business Insider," when disagreements or opposing viewpoints are stifled, or the parties involved are constantly battling, bullying is likely at play.

To determine what bullying is, and what it is not, the following distinctions should be made:

- Cautioning is not bullying, badgering is.

- Coaching is not bullying, humiliating is.

- Disciplining is not bullying, destroying is.

- Competition is not bullying, unhealthy competition is.

- Setting consequences is not bullying, making threats is.

- Holding people accountable is not bullying, seeking revenge is.

- Joking is not bullying, taunting is.

- Flirting is not bullying, stalking is.

- Being tough is not bullying, being mean is.

- Building endurance is not bullying, hazing is.

Cautioning vs. Badgering

Bullying should not be used as a sword or a shield. Managers who properly caution employees on performance, attitude or behavioral issues should not fear being labeled a bully.

Good bosses set high expectations and hold employees accountable for their performance, actions and behaviors. It is not bullying when expectations are clear, reasonable, attainable and fair, and employees are provided with the necessary resources, communication and support to achieve their goals. Bosses can be demanding and tough—that should not necessarily label them a bully.

Bosses who set unreasonable and unattainable expectations, and withhold resources, communications and support are bullies. Usually, they use harassment and badger people to perform—this is a form of exploitation and is bullying.

Disciplining vs. Destroying

Taking disciplinary action, up to, and including, discharge, is a critical part of effective performance management. When this action is taken with the intent to improve performance or correct behaviors or actions, it is not bullying. When this action is taken to set up a target, it becomes bullying. When targets fall into the bully's trap, they give bullies the ammunition they need to take disciplinary action—not to correct, but, as you have read in Vera's story, to destroy.

Throughout my career, I have had to invite many people out of the organizations I worked with. Dismissing an employee is one of the most difficult things a manager has to do, but it is critical to maintain the person's dignity. It never fails to amaze me how people are destroyed, not so much by this final act, but the method by which the action is taken. In August of 2013, when AOL Chief Tim Armstrong publicly fired Alel Lenz, the creative director of Patch (a division of AOL) on the spot, when Armstrong was addressing the unit's 1,100 employees, a new standard on how not to dismiss employees was established.

Coaching vs. Humiliating

To most readers, the misrepresentation will be obvious. A manager who publicly chastises an employee in front of coworkers, emphasizing the negative of the employee's performance, may defend himself with an assertion that he was coaching the employee. However, the bystanders and the target will probably perceive it for what it is—humiliation—and nothing more. Nothing has been taught; no coaching has taken place. The only result is bad feelings for everyone involved. The differences between coaching and humiliating are obvious. Even professional coaches can fall into this trap, heaping insult onto injury after a defeat. However, when true coaching wins over humiliation, the differential between gains and losses is enormous.

A coaching moment

Early in my career, I had the benefit of having a coach who influenced my management and leadership philosophy for life. Bob McCutcheon, a senior executive at Loblaw Companies Limited (Canada's largest food retailer), appeared in my office early one morning, sat down and took out his pipe (they allowed smoking in those days).

As he prepared his pipe (a long, drawn-out process), he started.

"Son I have a major problem. You see, there is a young manager; he is cocky, overly aggressive to the point of being abrasive, not sensitive to others, unreasonably demanding, doesn't listen to others, and bullies people to get things done." Flattered that Bob, who was considered the senior statesman, would come to me with such a weighty issue, I quickly said, "I would fire the SOB." After taking a long drag from his pipe, Bob responding by saying, "Well, son, that's my dilemma. You're the SOB I am talking about."

Thankfully, Bob did not follow my advice but, for me, it was a lifelong coaching lesson and I went on to become, at age twenty-nine, the youngest vice president with the organization and enjoyed a twenty-three year career with them.

Competition vs. Unhealthy Competition

Like conflict, competition is a fact of life. We live in a competitive society and it is not altogether a bad thing. Some competition is healthy and some is not.

Healthy competition celebrates excellence on either side. Healthy competition is motivated out of a love of the game or task, whatever it may be, and doing it well.

Bullying is often at play in unhealthy competition where beating others or being the best is the only goal, and the pressure to win is more important than the fun of playing or learning. Unhealthy competition celebrates victory over others, sometimes at any cost. Unhealthy competition is motivated out of a fear of losing.

How employees are measured, rewarded, recognized, and advanced, influences both healthy and unhealthy competition. For example, team goals, metrics, and rewards foster healthy competition; but heavily weighted individual goals, metrics and rewards risk unhealthy competition. Also, pitting employees against each other creates a risk of unhealthy competition.

An example of healthy competition in the workplace is one in which two teams face off to solve the same problem. At the end of the competition, the teams come together and share their solutions and processes. Competition such as this can lead to startling innovation as teams share and learn from each other and lift each other up.

An example of unhealthy competition in the workplace is groups or individuals pitted against each other for the approval of a boss. The two sides grow defensive of each other and focus on undermining the other as communication breaks down. Feelings of acrimony, hostility, and contempt are planted and the groups employ destructive tactics such as sabotage, gossip, and innuendo. They malign each other on the company intranet, and the efforts of the entire department suffer as a result.

An infamous illustration of unhealthy competition is the incident between U.S. Olympic Figure Skating teammates Tonya Harding and Nancy Kerrigan. In January of 1994, in a nefarious display of unhealthy competition, figure skating champion Nancy Kerrigan was literally taken out at the knees by the husband of her rival Tonya Harding, eliminating Kerrigan from the 1994 U.S. Figure Skating Championship. Tonya Harding was subsequently disgraced, and after bouts with alcohol and impaired driving charges, she took her demons into the ring by launching a boxing career.

Holding Accountable vs. Seeking Revenge

People should be held accountable for their words, actions, behaviors and performance. When retaliatory action is taken, it becomes revenge.

Consequences vs. Threats

There are good and bad consequences. To outline the consequences of an action or behavior is not bullying. When threats are used, e.g., "If you don't do this, you will be fired," it is bullying. An example of outlining a consequence is: "Breach of this policy could result in disciplinary action, up to and including discharge."

Joking vs. Taunting

The workplace should be a fun place to be. It is okay to poke fun at someone, and it is even more effective if you poke fun at yourself. Joking and teasing has to be a give and take—simply put, if you can't take it, don't give it.

One-time inappropriate and offensive comments said in jest are not bullying; it becomes bullying when the comments are repeated and used to offend, disparage, insult, demean and ridicule.

In Palm Beach in 2012, a former police captain challenged his demotion to officer. Two officers claimed that the captain created a hostile work environment by using slurs against women, Jews, racial minorities, gays, and people who are overweight. The offensive behavior is alleged to have occurred over a period of years and six people lodged discrimination and harassment complaints.

The captain's defense was that he was only joking and he has a "strong sense of humor."

A witness in his defense claimed, "He's a jovial and joking kind of guy. I've seen people go back and forth, but it is always smiles." It should be noted that this witness was not a target, and the people who were, did not see the humor.

During my career, I have dealt with a number of similar situations, and in most cases, the person accused rationalizes the behaviors as "just joking—did not mean to be harmful or malicious," and, in all of these cases, I found that they were guilty of bullying with the intent to hurt and harm.

Flirting vs. Stalking

Flirting is part of human nature, and it would be wrong and impossible to make it illegal in the workplace. Stalking, on the other hand, is harassing with unwanted and obsessive attention.

There is a line when flirting starts to become bullying. That line is when it is unwanted and, if the flirting continues, the stalking begins, and it is bullying. Most cases can be easily dealt with by the recipient of the flirting simply by saying something to the effect of, "I am flattered that you are giving me attention, but it makes me uncomfortable." This, unfortunately, does not always stop it when the person making the advancements has some power or control over the target.

Toughness vs. Meanness

"Nothing is more despicable than respect based on fear."
–ALBERT CAMUS

Tough bosses are often accused of being bullies; those who are tough and mean usually are bullies. By my definition, being tough is setting high, but reasonable, expectations and holding people accountable for their performance, behaviors, and actions. I consider myself a tough boss and, based on feedback received, I have garnered the respect of subordinates. The tough bosses who are mean are not respected—they are feared.

On Saturday, August 30, 2013, the *New York Times*, in an article by Jack Ewing titled "Top Banker's Image Clouded," reported the suicide of Pierre Wauthier, a 53-year-old chief financial officer of the Zurich Insurance Company in Switzerland. Zurich is one of the world's largest insurers. In a note written by Mr. Wauthier shortly before he died, he "blamed pressure from Mr. Ackermann (the chairman of Zurich) for his despair" and said that Ackermann "was forcefully trying to lift profits."

Mr. Ackermann resigned shortly after Mr. Wauthier's death. The *New York Times* reporter wrote: "Another way to view the story is that Mr. Ackermann was simply a top manager doing what top managers are supposed to do when a company is not performing as well as it should . . . and that it is possible that his suicide had more to do with personal demons than pressure brought to bear by Ackermann." I predict that many organizational leaders will take this view rather than internalize this tragedy and question whether their tactics could drive someone to such despair.

The May 2016 suicide of another Zurich senior executive further endorses the likelihood that the corporate culture at Zurich Insurance Company is so toxic as to be lethal. Martin Senn was another disgraced CEO who resigned in December of 2015 after failing to complete a desired acquisition. My challenge that Mr. Wauthier's suicide resulted from him dealing with "personal demons" is fortified by this additional tragedy. It must raise the question of what created those personal demons? In his own words, Mr. Wauthier blamed Ackermann for his despair. However, it appears that the poisonous culture extended beyond Mr. Ackermann and Is so pervasive that it survived him. As I indicated earlier, it is not a question of being tough; it is the method by which results are achieved that is the bullying, not the toughness.

Building Endurance vs. Hazing

In the section "Altering the Attitudes of Organizational Leaders," I use the Miami Dolphins harassment case to illustrate the distinction between building endurance and bullying. Hazing takes place in the workplace usually to initiate a new employee or degrade someone who is, or perceived to be, different. People who do the hazing rationalize it as harmless fun, which, in some cases may be true. However, when the target is degraded in any way through racial or homophobic slurs or forced to conduct disgusting acts, the only people who are having fun are the bullies and, sadly, the bystanders.

Bullying and Performance Management

Making Weak Management Strong

Ambiguity and subjectivity in performance management give managers a license to bully and discredit their subordinates. A host of European studies have found that many of the environmental characteristics that contribute to bullying actually describe the functional features of a work unit, and that most of them are also factors related to leadership style and supervisory practices. Heinz Leymann commented, in his article, "The Content and Development of Mobbing at Work," "that of the eight hundred cases studied where mobbing (bullying) occurred frequently, an almost stereotypical pattern of poorly organized working methods and weak management were found." Forcing someone out of an organization is the number one motivation that bullies have for targeting their victims. Bullies usually use poor performance and/or a poor attitude to build a case against their targets.

Without clear, fair, reasonable and measurable expectations, managers are left to their own devices to manage performance. Where there is a lack of systems to set and measure expectations, there is usually frustration.

Employees are frustrated because they are not sure what is expected of them or feel they are being taken advantage of if the manager sets unrealistic targets, or uses favoritism in the allocation of work, or uses the lack of a system to set the employee up to fail. This frustration also causes employees' attitudes to sour.

When this happens, the bystanders or coworkers also get frustrated. They are frustrated because they believe, or are conditioned to believe, that not everyone is pulling his or her weight and, if their attitude suffers, they are regarded as a complainer and/or troublemaker. Where the target falls into "a trap," the bystanders or coworkers usually side with the bully because the bully has proven that his target is a poor performer and/or has a bad attitude.

Without some form of performance management systems in place, poor quality managers will become frustrated as well and lash out at people who they believe are not meeting expectations.

Generally, employees at all levels respond well to clear expectations and enjoy working in high performance organizations. Being part of a winning team is a real motivator. The key to employees accepting, even embracing, clear and high expectations is that they be fair and attainable and be measurable. Predator bullies, however, resist performance management systems and attempt to manipulate them.

Systems, Practices and Measurement

There are various types of systems, including engineered labor standards. Which system is most effective largely depends on the type of operation and nature of the work. Most organizations have industry or sector benchmarks, best practice performance management systems, standards and targets available to them.

However, corporations must also beware of using systems, practices or measures that don't actually contribute to productivity and a positive culture. For example, many of the more creative and culturally exciting companies, such as start-ups and ad agencies, have cultures that promote—even demand—inordinately long work weeks.

In the case of agencies and law firms, it's because they profit from billable hours—the more hours they can bill, the more profitable they will be. For many start-ups, the mission is the siren's song: the itch they're there to scratch often creates cult-like enthusiasm, which is easily manipulated to the benefit of the owners.

A professor in the department of economics at Stanford University, John Pencavel, discovered that increasing hours offers diminishing returns.

As reported by Leah Eichler in *The Globe and Mail*, Pencavel said, "Successive increases in hours result in successively smaller increases in output," with output failing to increase at sixty-five hours a week.

Professor Pencavel determined that working a total of seventy hours a week delivered slightly less productivity than those who worked forty-eight hours per week.

"The point is that it may well not be in the interest of the employer to schedule hours at which output starts to increase so little," he said, unless, of course, you can bill for them.

Another popular metric used by corporations for hiring, promotion and management policies is the Myers-Briggs tests. However, there is little concrete scientific research to back up the use of this tool to determine an employee's abilities or fitness in any given corporation. The murky science and false sense of security tests such as this provide enables many corporations to use them to support biased goals. The absence of concrete cause-and-effect makes this a dangerous tool in the hands of someone eager to manipulate the system. This is not to say the tests have no value: they do. How they are used it what is, too often, questionable.

Another popular management system is the 360-review where employees are reviewed by their management, peers and subordinates. In a truly open and supportive business culture, this is a great way to receive useful feedback balanced, as it is, by supporters as well as detractors. However, in most, more toxic, business environments, this approach provides employees with a tool to sabotage others' careers with innuendo and trumped-up complaints. The higher one goes up the ladder—and the more difficult the management decisions—the more likely it is that some decisions will be unpopular, and some reviewers will have ambitions toward the higher position and want to unseat whomever holds it.

There is a myth that bullying legislation and/or anti-bullying policies restrict and limit managers from having open and honest conversations with their subordinates and that employees will abuse legislation and policies as a shield or a sword when they are challenged on performance or attitude issues. The reality is, without performance management systems in place, organizations are at risk of having employees use legislation and/or policies to lodge complaints that they are being bullied when they are challenged on performance. The other reality is, where there is an effective and fair performance management system in place, there are fewer complaints, regardless of existing legislation or policies.

Research suggests that overloaded and bullied employees tend to work for organizations that are declining or shrinking, where the management style is bureaucratic and reactive. In contrast, those employees who feel purposeful, energized and recognized are those who work for growing, dynamic companies where the management style is empowering and successful.

With an effective and fair performance management system in place, managers are able to have a positive discussion with their subordinates even when correcting deficiencies. Rather than lashing out, they are able to have a fact-based conversation that addresses what the employee needs to do to meet expectations or targets and how the manager can help them instead of threatening them.

One other factor to consider is the workers' position within the organization and the relative control they have over their work and/or their closeness to the success of their efforts. The journal *Sociology of Health & Illness* published a study linking depression and anxiety to middle management in August of 2015. The supposition is that those at the lower rungs of the professional hierarchy are closer to production and results, so see the concrete achievement of their efforts. Senior management sees the company growing and is well compensated; whereas, those in the middle too often are removed from the actual production and don't enjoy the financial and emotional benefits of senior management.

Women Do Not Need to Bully to Break through the Glass Ceiling

During my career, I have mentored a number of women as they advanced to managers and executives. As most organizations are still dominated by males, it is a challenge for women to break through the glass ceiling, and most of the women I worked with have had to fight their way to the top echelons of management.

Women are conditioned to be tough to progress (even survive) in male-dominated organizations. In many of these environments, women have to meet higher standards to prove their toughness than their male peers. As indicated earlier, being tough should not be considered a negative attribute. It is negative, however, when tough is paired with mean.

Clearly, a double standard exists; when a woman asserts herself, even if she is not a bully, she is very likely going to be called a bitch or be told that she is being emotional. When a man is tough, but not a bully, he usually garners respect and when he bullies, it is usually rationalized as "doing what he has to do to get things done." When women react to comments, situations, or actions they find offensive, people may comment, "If you can't take the heat, get out of the kitchen."

Bottom line, women have had to develop a thicker skin than men to advance, and in so doing, often fall into the bully's trap—in essence, becoming a bully who is targeted by another bully.

Based on my experience, there is a double standard as both the victim and the organization are less tolerant when women bully men than vice versa.

A dynamic commonly at play in women bullying women is the motive of eliminating a real or perceived threat. This commonly manifests in discrediting through gossip and innuendo or exclusion. Studies show that, when women who progress in an organization have less talent than some of their subordinates, it is frequently because they are viewed as tougher, have garnered favors or the subtle approval to bully from their bosses, or they have learned to manipulate the social fabric of the office to their own favor. These women often know they have less talent than the women they are excluding and view their bullying as the means to keep their positions, both professional and social. My observation is organizations that have implemented affirmative action programs or quotas have often promoted women with less talent than some of their subordinates.

Many women have told me that women will bully other women who are a direct threat to their bosses or men they admire in the organization.

One comment resonated greatly with women I have spoken to on the topic: "If there are two women in a board meeting and ten men, the two women will view each other as a greater threat rather than any of the men."

Sexual Bullying

"Welcome sexual harassment is an oxymoron."
–RICHARD POSNER

As there is an abundance of published material on sexual harassment and how it is defined, as well as its effects, there is no need for me to expand on what already exists. I will rather focus on the dynamics of sexual bullying in the workplace.

Like other forms of bullying, sexual harassment usually occurs between a boss and subordinate, and the person making the advancements has some power or control over the target.

In the many cases of sexual bullying I have dealt with over my career, most were women who were bullied by a boss who believed he was entitled by virtue of the position he held, knowing the target would be afraid to report. In most cases, threats or promises were made and, usually, sexual favors were sought in exchange for extra pay and/or promotions. While the majority of cases are male bosses bullying female subordinates, male and female bosses also target male subordinates for sexual favors.

Rush Limbaugh, the conservative talk show host, made this crude comment: "Some of these babes, I'm telling you, like the sexual harassment crowd, they are out there protesting what they actually wish would happen to them." This reflects an attitude that is far too prevalent in people of power. They assume that their subordinates, as Limbaugh asserts, desire their advances because of who they are.

The entertainment industry is riddled with stars whose sense of entitlement seems to spur inappropriate, illicit and illegal behavior. In the U.K., the recent revelation of Jimmy Savile and the BBC's apparent indifference and neglect to his crimes, the CBC's too-late investigation into Jian Ghomeshi's abuse of women, and the ongoing drama attached to Bill Cosby's transgressions in the U.S., demonstrate the ubiquity of the free pass given to stars when it comes to accountability—and that of those who profit off of them.

However, the issues are not limited to the entertainment industry. For example, Westjet Airlines faces a class action lawsuit for failing to create a safe work environment for female flight attendants. A corporate culture that promotes alcohol-fueled socializing during layovers, but failed to respond to repeated complaints about pilots who expected sexual favors during these layovers, is at the heart of the lawsuit. Once complaints were registered, the pilots were protected by the airline, citing "privacy protection," (and freeing them to assault unknowing victims), whereas, the complainants frequently saw their schedules curtailed and professional opportunities decline.

In August of 2013, Bob Filner resigned as mayor of San Diego as part of a sexual harassment settlement with his former press secretary Irene McCormack Jackson. After Jackson filed her suit, 17 others came forward also accusing harassment, including two women who had been raped while serving in the armed forces. Filner appears to be a serial sexual predator, which I have found to be true in the majority of cases I have dealt with. If one person comes forward and is found to be credible, you can bet that there are many others who have been assaulted by the predator.

On August 22, 2012, the *UK Telegraph* reported in an article by John-Paul Ford Rojas called "Bullying Seen as Acceptable in the Army" that every woman questioned in a survey conducted by an adjutant general was a victim of unwanted attention. The survey interviewed 6,000 of 25,000 service people under the general's command; 400 were women.

A U.S. Department of Defense report in 2012 indicated approximately 26,000 members of the military were sexually assaulted and, of these, 53 percent were attacks on men in which the majority of perpetrators identify themselves as heterosexual. Given the fear and shame factor in reporting, these numbers are understated and, like other forms of bullying, it is hard to capture the true scope and dimension of the issue.

Another dynamic of sexual bullying is that bullies frequently retaliate against anyone who rejects his or her advances. This is one of the primary reasons targets are afraid to report: rejecting an advance is seen as a career-killing move. The term "Hell hath no fury like a woman scorned." applies as much to men as it does to women. I can relate to this as I have been the target of vindictiveness because I rejected someone's advances, and it is one of the most disturbing experiences I have ever encountered.

Virginia Messick exemplifies how difficult it is for targets to report assault. She is one of sixty-two trainees who were victims of assault or other improper conduct by thirty-two instructors in 2011 at Lackland Air Force Base in San Antonio, Texas.

Virginia did not initially report being raped because protocol required that she report it to the person who attacked her.

This proves, not for the first time, that sometimes the cure can be as bad as, or worse than, the disease. Much of the financial community, for instance, insists that new hires sign an arbitration agreement, forcing all job-related claims to be settled in-house—typically by arbitrators hired and paid for by the company. This achieves two goals:

1. No details of claims—or settlements—will go public, limiting awareness, accountability and the court of public opinion.

2. The deck is stacked in favor of the company, preventing complainants from a truly fair hearing.

In addition to working harder to prevent sexual harassment—or bullying of any kind—organizations need to reconsider how they resolve claims from those brave enough to make them.

The ethic of reciprocity—Linda's story

Linda is a single mother who has worked as an Administrative Assistant for a not-for-profit agency for twelve years. Linda's boss Eric is the executive director who joined the agency after retiring as a senior executive with a major pharmaceutical firm.

Eric and Linda enjoyed an excellent working relationship, and Eric was sensitive and responsive to the pressures that Linda faced as a single mom and accommodated her when she needed to come in late or leave early to attend to her daughter.

Although Linda earned a decent wage, money was tight, she had a mortgage, her car was nine years old and repairs were starting to cost more than it was worth. Linda's ex was a dead beat and had not provided any financial support since they separated.

In late 2007, Linda was diagnosed with cancer. The prognosis was good; however, she required an operation and the drug regimen required her to miss work at least one week a month for eight to twelve months.

Linda's benefits with the agency did not include short-term disability and the drug therapy prescribed was not approved on the medical plan she purchased. Linda felt that there were few options. None of her family members had the capacity to support her through this, nor could her friends.

Desperate, Linda went to Eric and laid out the situation. Eric responded immediately by telling her not to worry, he would figure something out. "Your main focus has to be on getting better," he assured her.

The next day, Eric told her that she could take off as much time as she needed, with pay, and the agency would pay for her drug therapy, and if she required home care or someone to take care of her daughter while she was being treated, the agency would pay for this as well. Linda was so relieved that she jumped up and gave Eric a big hug.

In early 2008, the tumor was successfully removed and she started chemotherapy. The side effects were relatively moderate, yet, it did require that she be off work for six or seven days after each treatment.

During this period, Eric was wonderful. He not only delivered on his promises, he supported Linda emotionally as well, always asking how she was feeling, inquiring how her daughter was coping and telling her if there was anything else she needed, all she had to do was ask.

In March of 2008, Eric invited Linda out for dinner to discuss the agenda for the next board meeting. After going over the agenda, they exchanged stories about their backgrounds, families and friends. Eric confided that his marriage of forty-seven years was not a happy one and he was very lonely for companionship. When they went to their cars, Eric asked Linda if they could meet for dinner on a regular basis. While this raised a red flag with Linda, she agreed, thinking, "It's the least I can do after everything he has done for me."

For the next few weeks, Eric and Linda had dinner every week except the weeks when she was in treatment. Even though Eric was old enough to be her father, Linda enjoyed his company. He was caring, witty, and had the energy of a man twenty years his junior.

In May, Eric invited Linda to a conference in Atlanta. "It will be good for your professional development." Linda thought it was unusual for Eric to make the hotel arrangements but, once they arrived, she found out why. Checking in, Linda was aghast that Eric only arranged for one room they had to share. Once they got into the room, Linda objected. Eric became irritated and said, "You don't have a choice here. Have you never heard of the ethic of reciprocity?"

Linda was upset and confused, "What do you mean?" she asked.

"Let's face it, I am helping you and now you are going to help me," Eric answered. He continued by saying "You have a choice here. You can leave, but if you do, it's over, I will fire you."

It started that day. Linda had to submit to Eric's demands to save her job and continue to receive financial support for her condition. If she did not have her daughter to think about, she would have walked out. Linda also realized that, given the overall economic situation and her medical condition, she would not be able to find another job.

For a man in his early seventies, Eric had an insatiable appetite for sex and he became increasingly demanding, insisting that they get together at a sleazy motel at least twice a week. Linda's only reprieve was when she was in chemotherapy. Even then, he tried to convince her to meet. Also, Eric's tastes went from vanilla to kink.

This went on until November of 2009. Linda was at the breaking point. A number of times she almost called the chair of the board of the agency but decided against it as Eric and the chair were very close and Eric indicated that if she told anyone he would claim that she initiated "the affair."

In the last week of November, Eric drove Linda to a new location. They went into a building that looked like a warehouse.

Once they got inside, Linda discovered that it was a sex club. In the center of the room was a huge mattress with a number of people engaged in all kinds of revolting activities. "Here is the deal," Eric said, "we are going to check our clothing in the locker room, then I want you to join in the group, while I watch."

Linda had had enough, and she ran to the entrance and got out. Fortunately, she was able to grab a cab and asked the driver to take her home. Once she got home, Linda called the police who came over immediately.

Eric was charged with sexual assault and his case is still pending. The Board of Directors asked for, and received, his resignation.

Linda continues to work for the agency. Eric's replacement is a former board member and she and Linda have a good working relationship. Being a cancer survivor, the new executive director was able to relate to what Linda was going through medically; however, she, like others, could not imagine the horror Linda suffered by following Eric's distorted view of the "ethic of reciprocity."

Sexual Orientation and Bullying in the Workplace

Over the last decade, much progress has been made in shifting attitudes on sexual orientation. Notwithstanding the progress made, even in enlightened organizations, homosexual and transgender workers are fearful of either coming out or being outed.

This is not surprising as companies in 28 of the U.S. states can still fire a worker for being gay. With the exception of Apple's Tim Cook, there are no openly gay CEOs in Fortune 500 companies.

In 2007, BP PLC Chief John Browne resigned amid revelations he had lied in court about how he met his boyfriend. In a *Wall Street Journal* article on July 25, 2012, by Leslie Kwoh called "A Silence Hangs Over Gay CEOs" Browne stated, "Keeping executives from coming out are homophobic corporate cultures and boards" and "companies are very conservative and the bigger the business is, the more conservative it is."

Similarly, in professional sports, very few athletes have had the courage to come out. Mark Tewksbury, the Canadian Olympic Gold Medalist in swimming, stated at the 2009 Vancouver Q Hall of Fame launch, "It's a difficult place to be if you are not straight." "Sport is still a top down from policy makers," he told *Daily Xtra*, Canada's GLBT magazine, adding, "it's very dogmatic and rule-bound. People don't want to change rule structures. It's by nature highly conservative. It's pretty much the last machinations of the old-boys club."

Until Jason Collins, a veteran of 12 NBA seasons, announced in April of 2013 that he was gay, there were no openly gay athletes in the NHL, NBA, and MLB. The NFL made history in May of 2014 when Michael Sam was chosen by St. Louis and became the first openly gay draft pick. In soccer, Robbie Rogers, the former member of the U.S. National Team, revealed on his blog in February 2013 that he was gay. Had he announced earlier, he would have been the first openly gay male athlete to play in a major American team sport.

Very few in broadcasting have come out, a rare exception being CNN's Anderson Cooper who did so in July 2012.

In entertainment, a 2012 survey by the Actors Equity union revealed that only 57 percent of gay actors felt they could be open about their sexuality with their agent, and one-third had experienced homophobia in the workplace, saying it came from other performers.

CASE STUDY

No way out—Mark's story

Mark worked for a mid-sized medical equipment company for twenty-two years. He started as an inventory control clerk, working his way up and was promoted to head of purchasing. He joined the Midwestern company after graduating from the local community college. Mark and Lori married the year after he graduated college and had two sons who were in their late teens.

In 2009, Mark was found dead in his car, which was parked in his garage, from carbon monoxide poisoning. Mark had committed suicide.

While Mark's suicide came as a total shock to Lori and their sons, they knew there had been something wrong for a long time, but did not know what. For two or so years, Mark had not been himself. He was withdrawn, irritable, depressed, lethargic, suffered stomach disorders, headaches and was restless at night, unable to sleep. He kept to himself and, when asked what was going on, would always answer, "Nothing really, just a bit of pressure at work," and said there was nothing to worry about.

Shortly after the funeral, John, a close friend of Mark's, asked to meet with Lori, indicating that he had some information that she should be aware of that would answer why Mark had taken his life. John was very distraught and said "If I had done something earlier, Mark would be alive today." John said that Mark asked him to tell Lori the whole story after "he left."

John reported that Mark approached him a month before he died to ask for help, that he had no one else to turn to. Mark said he had done something terrible and needed to make it right and he had to get out of the situation he found himself in. Based on what Mark told him, John assumed that "getting out" meant that Mark was going to run away.

Mark and his manager Ed, who was also a long-term employee, had a reasonable working relationship but were not close socially. Ed was pretty rough around the edges and could be crude when things upset him. Mark learned to live with it and rationalized Ed's behavior with, "Oh, that's just Ed."

In early 2006, Ed said, "I hear you are a f—ing faggot. Somebody told me that you are a regular at some queer joint called the Red Rooster." (The Red Rooster is a gay establishment in a neighboring city.)

Mark was flabbergasted and said, "I don't know what you are talking about, and even if I was, it is none of your business." Ed then pulled out three photos and said, "You're not only a f—ing faggot but you're a f—ing liar. You work for me and it is my f—ing business."

Mark was devastated. Not only did he risk losing his family should his sexuality become known, he feared for his physical safety. Homosexuals have lost their lives. Only a decade earlier, Matthew Shepard, a young man from Wyoming, was beaten and left for dead hanging on a barbed wire fence after frequenting a gay bar.

The information floored Mark. He asked, "Who else knows?"

Ed smiled and said "I always knew you were a pansy, so I decided to have you followed. The only other person is a private investigator who is paid to keep his mouth shut." Ed then proceeded to tell Mark that he had a little scheme in mind and, if Mark wanted "Our little secret" kept that way, he would have to play along.

During his high school years Mark knew he was attracted to men, but resisted the temptations and felt that it was a phase. In grade 12 he started dating Lori. The city they lived in was small, fairly close knit and there were no opportunities for Mark to explore what he came to realize was not a passing phase. Mark was as closeted as one could be.

Ten or so years after Mark and Lori married, Mark attended a conference in Atlanta. He met John there, who, coincidentally, was from the same city and an alumnus of the college Mark attended. Mark and John recognized each other and decided to have dinner. Over dinner, they realized a mutual attraction and spent the remainder of the conference together. John was also married at the time and, while not as closeted as Mark, kept his sexuality a secret. Mark and John carried on an affair for fewer than two years and decided to end it, but remained close friends. John was the only person

Mark could be "out" with and John introduced him to "the scene" in the neighboring city.

After the confrontation with Ed, Mark was petrified. Mark was convinced that, if he were exposed, he would lose everything: Lori would leave him, his sons would disown him, it could kill his ailing parents, he would be shunned by the community, and Ed would find a way to force him out of the company.

Ed was already in Mark's office the next morning waiting for him. "Let's go for a ride," Ed suggested. Ed laid out the "scheme." "I will keep our little secret if you arrange for ten of our vendors to give us kickbacks. If you don't, I will go to my boss and tell him that you approached me with the idea to keep me quiet, because you found out I knew you were a faggot." Mark had Ed stop the car and threw up what little he had eaten for dinner the night before. What Ed was demanding went totally against Mark's value system. He prided himself on the relationships he developed with the vendor community and now he was being blackmailed to betray the company he loved, the vendor community, and himself.

"I can't do it," Mark declared.

"You don't have much of a choice, pansy boy; if you don't, you are going to be fired, and everyone will find out that you are a faggot who tried to keep it a secret by bribing me to do something illegal. Nobody will hire you again. I'll see to it that you will be on the street."

"Give me a couple of days to think about it," Mark asked.

"Take your time, faggot," Ed responded.

Mark did not know what to do. He considered discussing it with Lori, but he couldn't risk it. The only person he could talk to was John. Mark seriously considered suicide, but decided that was a coward's way out.

Two days later, Ed was waiting for Mark in his office. "Let's go for another ride," Ed suggested. This time, they drove to the local gym that they both belonged to. They met in the dry sauna where they could be alone.

"Now here is how it works, I will give you the names of ten vendors who I know will co-operate. All you have to do is give them an amount to deposit each month in an offshore account, and each month, you will transfer the entire balance to another offshore account. I will give you instructions on how and where to open the account and the instructions on how to automatically have the balance in your account transferred to my account."

It started that week. Mark met with each vendor in a safe environment and they all agreed to the terms. Mark knew that this type of thing went on but had no idea, based on the reaction of the vendors, that it was almost expected. It was obvious to Mark that he was not the first person Ed recruited to engage in this activity. Mark always wondered how Ed could afford to live in a multimillion-dollar house, with a stay-at-home wife, expensive cars and exotic trips. Now he knew. He also wondered if the higher-ups in the company questioned Ed's extravagant lifestyle.

The other thing that perplexed Mark was the lack of checks and balances in place. All an auditor would have to do is a net/net price comparison and it would show that they were overpaying for many items.

For close to three years, Mark's life was a living hell. Not only was he engaged in illegal activity, which, if he was caught, would land him in jail for a long time, but at every opportunity, when no one was within ear shot, Ed would call him a "f—ing faggot" or "pansy boy." Ed would also question Mark about his relationship with Lori and offer to "service her," as "obviously she is not getting it from you."

Ed became greedier and greedier. Periodically, Ed would arrange for them to meet in the dry sauna at the gym, again to make sure no one could listen, and make sure Mark was not wired. Even though Ed was a boorish goon, he was not stupid. At these meetings, Ed would add to the vendor list and increase the amounts the others were paying. The total amount collected over this period exceeded seven million dollars.

From the beginning, Mark kept a diary of every discussion he had with Ed and the vendors. He also had a record of each transaction. At some point, he was going to expose Ed. The only problem is he did not know how.

Finally, he figured it out. He would engage his friend, John. They met at John's house and Mark laid out the full story, giving John a copy of his diary and a record of all of the transactions. Mark indicated to John that "there was only one way to end this, I have to leave." John tried to convince Mark that he should go to the CEO of the company with this, to which Mark replied, "I just can't face him; this is my only way out."

Mark asked John to meet with Lori, "after I leave," and tell her the whole story. Mark indicated he wanted it to be Lori's decision whether to go to the CEO of the company with the diary and the records.

A month later, Mark got out.

Lori quietly listened to the whole story. "Now it all makes sense," she commented. "I knew from the beginning, that Mark was bisexual," she told John. "I also knew the two of you had a thing going, but I still loved him, we were best friends, had a wonderful relationship, and he was a great dad." Lori also indicated that she knew being bi or gay was not a choice, the choice was whether to be out or not and Mark had made his choice. Lori respected it because she knew that Mark believed if he came out it would hurt her and their sons.

Lori decided, after consulting with her sons, who wholeheartedly concurred, that she and John needed to go to the CEO of the company and relay the full story.

At the meeting, the CEO listened to the story, read the diary and reviewed the records of the transactions. When he finished, he wept and said, "I don't know how Mark was able to bear this burden for as long as he did. Lori, I am so ashamed of what happened here and that Mark did not feel comfortable enough to come to me with this.

"I would like to have a week to decide what to do," the CEO said, adding that he wanted to meet with Lori and John again after the week. He also gave them an assurance that Mark's name and reputation would be protected in whatever action they decided to take.

That week, the CEO met with the Chair of the Board of Directors and the Chair of Audit, gave them the full story and offered his resignation, which they refused, and they indicated that they, too, had to accept some responsibility for not having checks and balances in place.

As promised, the CEO met with Lori and John the following week to outline what the board had decided. A forensic audit was conducted that found that the kickbacks dated back to two years after Ed started with the company. Ed was charged, convicted, sent to prison, and ordered to make full restitution.

All of the vendors involved avoided criminal charges by making full restitution and paying the company penalties for their actions.

The CFO's resignation was accepted. The CEO and the board viewed him as being negligent. Checks and balances were put in place and periodic audits are now conducted to prevent this from happening in the future.

Lori continued to receive Mark's compensation until he would have reached retirement age, after which, she will receive his full pension benefits. Mark and Lori's sons will receive full scholarships to a university of their choice from the company.

Mark's reputation was protected.

What People Go through when They Fall into the Bully's Trap

As I outlined in the Introduction, bullies are masters of deflection, who deceive and manipulate to achieve their end. Their intent is to break the target down to become what they want them to be, which, in most cases, is a problem employee, and/or the villain. When this happens, the target falls into a very calculated trap.

People who are targeted usually go through four stages:

1. Denial and Rationalization

2. Deterioration

3. Paying the Price

4. Closure

Stage 1: Denial and Rationalization

While people who are targeted realize that something is out of the norm, most do not identify it bullying. The initial reaction usually is to blame themselves, thinking—"I must have done something wrong" and believe that what they are experiencing will pass if they keep their heads down. Also, in most incidences, they attribute the behavior of the bully to be a matter of style, versus a calculated plan to destroy them, even when the bullying persists over time. Another common rationalization is the assumption that bullying behavior is "just the way it is around here and complaining about it will be viewed as a sign of weakness." Rarely do people confide in others about what they have to endure again because they do not want to be viewed as weak and unable to cope.

It is at this stage where targets are vulnerable to being bullied, particularly in those cultures that view bullies as heroes, and the bullying behaviors are a means to survive and advance.

Stage 2: Deterioration

As the bullying continues, and the target deals with it alone, it starts to affect the physical and emotional well-being of the target. They are under incredible stress, particularly if they feel that their job may be at risk. In the chapter called "Workplace Bullying and Post Traumatic Stress Disorder," I discuss how people entrapped by persistent bullying suffer from Post Traumatic Stress Disorder (PTSD). An astounding 95 percent of targets suffer from PTSD.

At this stage, the deterioration in performance and attitude becomes evident. This is all part of the bully's calculated plan. The target at this stage starts taking out his or her frustrations on others, at work and at home, withdrawing from outside interests and, in many instances, becoming dependent on alcohol or drugs to cope. The target is now fully in the bully's trap, and the bully has the ammunition needed to "appropriately deal with him."

Stage 3: Paying the Price

The bully, armed with ammunition, will, at this stage, force the issue. The target is wounded, weak, alienated and alone. The bully wants the target gone and will try to get the target to quit or do something that allows him to fire for cause.

Stage 4: Closure

Being targeted is something that very few people can get closure on. They replay what has gone on over and over without being able to let it go. For some, it leads to a total breakdown and, as you will see in the chapter called "Costs, Liabilities And Deadly Consequences," the only way to get closure is suicide, or for others, it is "going postal" and killing others.

Some seek closure through revenge. The following is a case study called "Seeking Revenge—Dean's Story" of an executive who was forced out by a bully. His revenge was helping employees become unionized, providing the competition with confidential information and discrediting the company with key clients, all of which resulted in the company going down. While I do not condone his actions, based on what I have experienced and what I have heard from others, it is completely understandable that a person would reach this breaking point.

Beyond the obvious costs and risks of bullying, the risk of losing reputation and brand value should be a major consideration for organizational leaders. Employees who are targeted may not seek revenge to the extent that is illustrated in the following case study, though the likelihood that they will speak badly of the organization is high.

Seeking revenge—Dean's story

Dean was a vice president of Operations for a waste management company in western Canada, a position that he held for just over nine years. In 2010, the company was sold to a multinational corporation and they appointed Mary as president and CEO. Mary had been with the multinational corporation for a number of years.

From the outset, Mary made it clear to Dean that, unless he significantly reduced operating costs, she would replace him. Dean felt that, while there were opportunities to reduce costs, an investment in new equipment and technology would be required to reduce many of the manual processes. The previous owners were reluctant to make the required investments and the company fell behind in benchmark comparisons to similar companies, including their competitors.

Mary's response to Dean was "We are not going to invest another dime in this company—make do with what you have, force your people to work harder, and threaten them with outsourcing if they don't comply." Dean tried to reason with Mary, who said, "If you can't do it, I will find someone who can."

Dean spent the next few months trying to improve the processes and looked for every avenue to reduce costs. Through his motivating skills, he engaged employees to find ways to improve their productivity. Although this yielded results, they were not enough to satisfy Mary. For almost nine months, Mary harassed Dean 24/7: she singled him out in meetings, berating him for putting the company at risk of closure because he was not reducing costs fast enough, called him at home after hours, on weekends and holidays, demanding to know what he was doing.

The breaking point for Dean was a call he received from Mary on New Years Day of 2011, when Mary demanded that Dean fire 10 percent of the workforce the next day. Dean told Mary that she was "crazy" and wanted an audience with Mary's boss. On the call, Mary fired Dean for insubordination. After some persuading, Dean's request for a meeting with Mary's boss was granted. The he was told that Mary was a star performer who always came through with the numbers.

Dean wanted revenge. A month after he was fired, he contacted a union official and worked undercover to recruit employees to join the union, which they did in record time. At the same time, he went to the company's major competitors and gave them classified information. He also went to one of the major clients whose contract with the company was up for renewal and indicated that the company was at risk and they would be better advised to go to the major competitor—which they did. Six months after Dean was fired, the company declared bankruptcy.

CASE STUDY

"The target becomes the bully"— Janet's story

In 2009, Janet, a registered nurse with more than twenty years of service, transferred to a new hospital within her municipality.

While Janet knew most of the nursing staff at the hospital, she rarely socialized with them, wanting to separate her work from her personal life and avoid the political dynamics she encountered in other hospitals.

Although there were many aspects of nursing that Janet did not like, the joy of easing the suffering of her patients negated the negatives.

Shortly after she joined, Janet observed a number of instances where Judy, one of her colleagues, verbally abused elderly patients and, in some instances, used undue physical force. Janet confronted Judy, who told her to mind her own business. The abuses by Judy continued and Janet confidentially lodged a complaint with the head nurse. The head nurse went to Judy and told her another nurse had lodged a complaint. Judy said she knew it was Janet who squealed on her and told the head nurse that Janet was a troublemaker and a loner who did not get along with anyone.

For three months after lodging the complaint, all of Janet's colleagues, including the head nurse, shunned her. The head nurse, who it turned out was a close friend of Judy's, started disciplining Janet for becoming too attached to the patients because she was doing things over and above what was required to make her patients comfortable. When Janet protested, the head nurse accused her of undermining her authority. When Janet went to Human Resources to complain, she was told nothing could be done and sided with the head nurse by indicating the extras that Janet gave to patients were not necessary and cost the hospital money.

Janet decided to take matters into her own hands and started gossiping to other nurses about Judy and the head nurse, relaying that Judy was abusing patients and the head nurse was condoning it because Judy and the head nurse were lesbians. Janet was disciplined by the hospital and the College of Nurses for this and almost lost her license to practice because of her actions. Janet became a bully who was targeted by another bully and she, not her tormentors, paid the price.

What Motivates Bullying

As you have seen in Part One, most organizations allow, condone, encourage, and even expect their managers to bully.

My research and that of others shows that the main reason people are targeted is to force them out.

The usual motivations and intentions are:

- To reduce labor costs

- Retaliation to punish the target

- Bigotry

- Exploitation—to get people to work harder and faster (it is the only way weak managers know how to manage)

- To exercise (abuse) their power

- To eliminate a threat

Reduce Labor Costs

Almost every day, we hear in the media about questionable business practices. One area that needs to be exposed is organizations using bullying tactics to reduce employment costs. Older workers and long-term employees are particularly vulnerable. The formula is very simple; force senior employees out and replace them with younger ones at a lower pay rate, thereby reducing the average salary. If anyone quits, severance is avoided. By doing this, there is an added incentive for those companies with a benefits plan: their pension costs and unfunded liability is greatly reduced. While I do not want to debate the false economics of this, I only want to expose it for what it is: ethically and morally dishonest and wrong.

Precedence could be based on the outcome of two class action suits that Federal Express faced. The two suits claim that FedEx has actual policies and practices in place designed to push employees out before they reach age fifty-five. The plaintiffs in the case allege that FedEx discriminates against couriers over forty years old, especially if they have more than ten years' seniority, by taking away their routes and setting unrealistic performance targets, and that the company gave supervisors lists of older workers to target for increased supervision, discipline, and harassment.

In 2015, more than 20,000 age-discrimination complaints were filed at the U.S. Equal Employment Opportunity Commission; sadly, very few have gone to court. Recent Supreme Court rulings make it challenging for employees to claim age discrimination because they must prove that age was the motivating factor. In addition, they denied money damages in cases against state agencies.

Studies have found that for more than 70 percent of the bullying targets, the only way to stop the bullying was to leave their employment.

Retaliation

While many employers claim to have an open-door policy and tools in place, such as a whistleblower hot line, not all welcome contrary viewpoints and reports of irregularities or wrongdoing. Some shoot the messenger and retaliate against employees who don't follow the party line, who fight an injustice, or report irregularities or wrongdoing.

My experience with companies with whistleblower hot lines is that executives and boards are proud of how few calls are made to the hotline without considering that employees and vendors may not trust the system.

In 2010, retaliation surpassed race discrimination as the most common type of charge filed with the U.S. Equal Employment Opportunity Commission (EEOC).

Even in the United States, which lags behind all westernized jurisdictions on anti-bullying legislation, the Supreme Court changed the grounds on which retaliation claims are actionable. With the Burlington Northern vs. White decision of the U.S. Supreme Court (2006), increased action is likely. With this decision, the court effectively broadened the allowable standard in retaliation claims made against employers.

The demise of organizations and the global meltdown could have been avoided had people in the know reported the wrongdoing. They did not, largely for fear of being retaliated against. In most cases, the whistleblowers are viewed as traitors and subject to bullying as punishment for their crime.

In almost 10,000 cases reported on the U.K. National Workplace Bullying Advice Line, the fifth reason for being bullied is "blowing the whistle on malpractice fraud, breaches of rules, regulations and procedures, or raising health and safety issues."

Robert Damon, formerly of Korn Ferry, was a high-level executive fired for whistleblowing against Korn Ferry's Chief Executive, Gary Burnison, who was allegedly mistreating several female colleagues. This parallels what I went through when I blew the whistle on a senior executive. Mr. Damon was then smeared with horrendous accusations by Korn Ferry in an attempt to discredit him, which is a typical tactic used against whistleblowers who sue for wrongful termination—something I had to fight for 18 months. The settlement that Korn Ferry ultimately agreed to suggests that their case was not as pristine as they claimed. Because of the gag orders associated with the settlement, we will never know all of the details of this case, but the ability of women to succeed at the organization long-term should tell the tale.

Bigotry

Despite the millions that organizations spend on diversity and sensitivity training, bigotry and hatred is still evident.

In 2015, Business in the Community, in partnership with YouGov.com, heard from 24,457 people working in the U.K. regarding racial equality in the workplace. Here are some of the findings:

- 28 percent of all BAME (Black, Asian and minority ethnic) employees witnessed or experienced harassment or bullying from managers within the last five years.

- 32 percent have witnessed or experienced harassment or bullying from colleagues.

- 48 percent of BAME employees feel they have been overlooked for promotion, whereas, only 23 percent of white employees feel the same.

- Organizations with greater racial diversity on senior teams experience 35 percent greater financial returns.

Exploitation and Weak Management

"All cruelty springs from weakness."
—SENECA

A host of European studies found that many of the environmental characteristics that contribute to bullying actually describe the functional features of a work unit, and most of them are also factors related to leadership style and supervisory practices. Heinz Leymann commented in his article, "The Content and Development of Mobbing at Work," that, of the 800 case studies where mobbing (U.K. term for bullying) occurred frequently, an almost stereotypical pattern of poorly organized working methods and weak management was found.

Research suggests that overloaded and bullied employees tend to work for organizations that are declining or shrinking, where the management style is bureaucratic and reactive.

When people fall into the bully's trap, they become like Vera in Vera's story: a poor performer with an attendance problem and bad attitude. This gives the bully the ammunition to take disciplinary action, up to, and including, discharge. This is a huge Catch-22 for the target and a huge enabler for the bully.

Kaj Bjorkqvist, Karin Osterman, and Monika Hjelt-Back in "Aggression Among University Employees" wrote: "Like domestic violence, it can be difficult for people to talk about workplace bullying."

This has made it difficult to capture the true dimensions of the problem, and helps explain why it is not always recognized. Like any abusive relationship, people tend to deny or minimize abuse as a way to survive it. The workplace provides a further wrinkle in that bullying behavior can be easily concealed by, or disguised as, "strong management." Likewise, it is difficult for targets to report, as targets risk retribution and job loss. It can also have a stigmatizing effect, since to admit to being harassed at work is something others might see as a weakness or an inability to cope.

Abuse of Power

"Power over a man's subsistence is power over his will."
—ALEXANDER HAMILTON

People who have power and have to rely on their position to get others to do things or not do things are bullies, and this is abuse of power, particularly if people are forced into doing things that are unethical or in conflict with their values and beliefs.

In the media, reports of corruption by executives and politicians have become commonplace. What is common in most of the stories we hear about is how long the corruption has gone on without people in the know coming forward. There is little question that these people were bullied into silence.

In organizations where there are no checks and balances, bullies can and do target employees purely to assert their power. Again, 70 percent of bullying is boss to subordinate—and the boss has the power of position and is in a position to use power to instill fear.

Although it happens that coworkers bully their colleagues, it is more often top down. When it starts at the top, it does impact the entire organizational culture.

Eliminating a Threat

Many bullies are insecure despite their confident facade. When bullies feel their power or status is threatened by a coworker or subordinate, they will not hesitate to target them.

During my career, I have been involved in a number of reorganizations. As reorganizations usually involve massive change—they also usually trigger reactions from those who fear losing power and control.

They wanted to push me out— William's story

In 2007, William quit his job as a driver for a major transportation and logistics company after twelve years of employment. At the time, William was forty-three years old. William thought that he would have no problem finding another job; however, with the economic downturn and the unemployment rate in southern California reaching double digits, this was not the case.

Until 2006, William thought that he would be a lifer with the company. The company provided good wages and benefits and had a pension plan. Working conditions were excellent and the vehicles were always clean and in good working order. The company prided itself on their employee relations and wanted to be known as "an employer of choice." They had a huge Human Resources department and all of the "state-of-the-art" employment policies, procedures and practices. A union represented the majority of employees.

In 2006, the company negotiated a new collective agreement with the union. The main changes were a two-tier wage and benefit structure, and a change in the pension plan from a defined benefit to a defined contribution. Existing employees maintained their wage grid and benefit coverage and had the option of switching their pension to the defined contribution plan. New hires would go on the new grid, the much-reduced benefit plan, and the defined contribution pension plan.

Almost immediately after the new collective agreement went into effect there was a major restructuring at the supervisory level and Geoff, a twenty-eight-year-old with an accounting background became William's boss. William's former boss, who was in his mid-fifties, not yet eligible for early retirement, was laid off. It turned out that most mid-level supervisory, managerial, administrative, and professional employees who were over age forty with ten or more years of service got caught up in the restructuring.

A few years earlier, the company had installed a very sophisticated truck routing system that made the loads and multiple deliveries efficient. The system featured engineered labor standards (a system to measure productivity), that is, the time it would take to make all of the deliveries. The system was very flexible in that it factored in traffic patterns at various times of the day and week. The system also allowed the company to give customers a fairly tight window of time when to expect their deliveries. Until William started working for Geoff, with few exceptions, he met or exceeded the standards set out by the system. The few exceptions were when traffic was unusually heavy or there were delays due to road closures. William and his coworkers felt the system was fair and it allowed them to earn bonuses for meeting and exceeding the standards.

A few weeks after Geoff started, he met with William to get to know him. Geoff asked William to go over his routine. "It's pretty basic really, I clock in, go to the dispatch office to get my schedule of deliveries, do a circle check of the truck for safety compliance, scan the bar code of each item to make sure that everything is accounted for and then I am on my way." Geoff asked how long this all took, to which William replied that he could usually be on the road within half hour. "Isn't that a bit long?" William said, "The system doesn't think so." Geoff responded, "It is my understanding that the system is a guideline, and I think you should be able to cut it in half." William said he would try to do it quicker.

Geoff checked every day for the next two weeks and, while William shaved off a few minutes, it still averaged out to the half hour. After two weeks, Geoff said, "You are not trying very hard, are you?" to which William replied, "I'm doing the best I can." Geoff became very agitated and indicated that he was going to keep a close eye on William and that he felt William was not measuring up to other drivers, who exceeded the standards more often than he did.

After this confrontation, William started having real difficulty meeting the standards, at least three times per week for the next four weeks, he ran over schedule, and the deliveries exceeded the delivery window.

Every time this happened, Geoff berated William, often in front of the dispatcher and other drivers. After four weeks, William went to John, his union representative, and told him what was happening. John said, "William, if you are not meeting standards, they have the right to go after you."

The following week, William was called to a meeting with Geoff, John and a Human Resource person. William was given a written warning to improve his performance or face further disciplinary action, up to, and including, discharge.

Over the next number of weeks, William pushed as hard as he could, took as many shortcuts as he could, stopped doing the circle check of his truck, went over the speed limits, and hurried through each delivery. There was no time for any small talk with the customers, and yet, while there was improvement, there were still an unacceptable number of times he was not able to meet the standards.

During this time, he noted that a number of other drivers were having the same difficulties; in fact, four had recently been fired for poor performance. William and some of his coworkers started to compare notes and discovered that all of the new hires had no trouble meeting the standards and most of the senior drivers were not. One of the senior drivers asked, "Do you think they are overriding the system?" The thought had occurred to William (drivers have a lot of time to think), and he decided to meet with John again to lay out this possibility.

John said he would request an audit of the system. This occurred a week later and the Industrial Engineer validated that the system was fair and that it did not appear that it was being tampered with.

Over the next three months, Geoff continually berated William, and two more disciplinary meetings were held. At the second meeting, Geoff indicated that unless there was significant improvement in the next two weeks, he would have no choice but to fire William. During this time, six more senior drivers left; some were fired, others quit.

There was no significant improvement. John called William and advised him to resign, as, otherwise, he would be fired and the union would not be able to protect him. He also pointed out that William would have far more difficulty finding another job if he were fired. William submitted his resignation the next day, giving two weeks' notice. Geoff accepted William's resignation and told him he would be paid for the two weeks, but he did not have to come in.

All of this made no sense to John and he wondered why none of the new hires had difficulty and almost all of the senior drivers did. John then checked with the Industrial Engineer to make sure the system had integrity. The Industrial Engineer took great offence and said, "I told you it was; who are you to question my professional ability?" John thought the response was a bit extreme, he was just checking to be sure.

A few weeks later, at a quarterly union meeting, John relayed what was happening to the senior drivers at his location. Every union representative John spoke to indicated the exact same thing was happening at his or her location.

"Remember, after the last set of negotiations, the company restructured and they laid off people with a lot of service?" one of the union representatives asked, adding, "Do you think that they are doing the same thing to the drivers?" Then it registered with John, thinking that, with the two-tier compensation structure, it was certainly an incentive for the company to get rid of more senior people and, if they got them to quit, it was like winning a trifecta at a horse race; they avoided paying severance, reduced their average hourly rate, and reduced their unfunded pension liability.

John, with the help of union representatives at a number of other locations, compiled a list of people who quit or were fired since the new agreement went into effect. They found that there was indeed a pattern. Ninety percent were over age forty with over ten years service. One of the representatives suggested that John approach one of the new supervisors brought in by the company who left shortly after joining.

Fred was a twenty-six-year-old who, after leaving the company, worked for an automotive supply firm. Like Geoff, Fred had an accounting background. Fred initially was reluctant to speak with John as, when he left the company, they insisted he sign a confidentiality agreement and breaching it could leave him open to a lawsuit. The head of Human Resources who conducted Fred's exit interview also implied that if Fred were to expose the company in any way, he would be blacklisted for years. Although Fred was concerned about speaking to John, his conscience dictated that the story had to come out. Too many people were having their lives' destroyed and it needed to be stopped. John and Fred met at a safe location and Fred relayed his experience.

Fred's first assignment was to learn the truck routing and standards system and then how to override it. After three weeks of intensive one-on-one training, he was assigned to a location and became a supervisor. Two weeks later, his manager gave Fred a list of sixteen drivers who, in the manager's words, "were troublemakers and needed to be forced out of the company." The manager indicated that Fred's number-one priority was to get them out. There was also a financial incentive involved: for every driver on the list who quit, Fred would receive a bonus of $6,000 and, for every driver who was fired, $3,500. The reason for the difference was the fired drivers would likely get severance.

The method he used to force the drivers out was to alter the standard to an impossible-to-achieve level. The important thing was to phase this in for each driver on the target list so it would not be obvious. Once a trend of "not meeting standards" was established, Fred was to go after the driver and harass them to the point they quit. The manager indicated that the union's staff Industrial Engineer could audit the system without a worry as "he is in our hip pocket."

Initially, Fred played along, but soon he realized that the drivers on the list were not the troublemakers the manager described, but decent hard workers who were targeted in a systemic way so that the company could significantly reduce their labor costs. This was totally contrary to Fred's value system and he resigned.

Fred insisted on an exit interview with the head of Human Resources and relayed the story to her. As indicated earlier, Fred was warned to keep quiet.

John prepared a report and met with the president of the union. The staff Industrial Engineer was confronted and confessed that he was paid off by management to validate the integrity of the system. In exchange for a signed and witnessed affidavit, he was allowed to resign, which protected his retirement benefits.

A grievance was filed on behalf of every driver targeted who either quit or was fired following the new collective agreement. The union is also in discussions with similarly targeted employee groups to convince them to file a class action suit against the company. (As the union didn't represent these groups, they were unable to file a grievance.)

Predictably, the company denied any wrongdoing and vigorously fought the filed grievance.

At the time of this writing, William was still out of work. Recently, he and his family moved in with his in-laws as the home they lived in for eight years went into foreclosure. There is a bit of income coming in from William's wife, who works part-time for a national drug chain. There is some hope that William may be able to get his job back and be paid for the period he has been off.

CASE STUDY

Exploitation—Leila's story

Leila never wanted to leave the Philippines. Married, with two small children, she and her husband struggled financially to make ends meet. A nurse by training, Leila and her husband, a construction worker, found themselves in and out of the workforce due to the country's high rate of unemployment and poverty. When they were both working, they barely made enough money to pay the rent on a small one-bedroom apartment in Manila, let alone buy a house where the family could raise their children properly.

Leila's sister worked as a nanny in Canada. When Leila found herself out of work for nearly six months, and her husband lost his job, she decided to apply to work abroad as well. It was a tough decision, as she knew she would be leaving her two small children, ages four and two. But she promised to write every day and return for visits every year.

Leila knew from her sister and friends working in Canada that she could earn as much as $1,200 a month, three times as much as she earned in the Philippines. She would send all of her salary home to support her husband. Leila also discovered, during a training course to work as a caregiver in Canada, that, after two years of employment, she could apply for permanent Canadian residency, essentially, citizenship. She began to dream of offering her children better lives and access to good Western schools and universities. She also dreamed of becoming a nurse in Canada when she completed the Live-in Caregiver Program (LCP). The LCP states that a nanny must complete two years of full-time employment within a three-year period. While in the LCP, the caregiver must live in her employer's home.

It took six months for Leila to complete a required training program in Manila, which taught her basic care-giving skills that she already knew from nursing. She then paid an employment agency the equivalent of $2,000, which she borrowed from a bank, to find her a placement in Canada. Finally, her employer, a wealthy woman in Vancouver, British Columbia, agreed to sponsor Leila under the LCP to work as her nanny. The woman, Rita, had five children, ranging in age from four to sixteen. Leila would be responsible, or so the letter of employment stated, for looking after the children only.

Leila said her painful goodbyes and left for Canada. She arrived in Vancouver on an unusually snowy day in January. From the get-go, Leila encountered one problem after another. Her employer didn't pick her up at the airport for nearly three hours. Leila waited in the terminal, impatiently pacing back and forth. The telephone number given to her by her employment agency didn't work. Leila had no way of reaching her new boss. When her new employer did arrive, she said she had to run some errands before taking Leila to the house. Leila, who was tired due to the long flight and the time difference, was put to work right away, preparing a dinner for the entire family and cleaning up before she was able to even unpack.

Her days unfolded much the same. Leila had to be up and working by 6 a.m., preparing breakfasts and lunches for the children for school. The youngest, age four, only attended kindergarten half a day, so Leila was responsible for caring for him in the mornings. After she walked the older children to school, she had to clean the dishes, do laundry, vacuum and clean the washrooms, all the while looking after the four-year-old. None of the children did chores and were not neat. Leila found herself cleaning their rooms. She then had to make two dinners: one for the children and another for her employers, who ate later. Often, she was not finished cleaning the dinner dishes and kitchen until nine or ten at night. Her employers also had dinner parties every week, for which Leila had to cook and serve. Leila found herself working seven days a week, from about 6:00 a.m. until 9:00 p.m.

If this wasn't bad enough, Leila then learned that her employer was docking room and board from her salary. Leila would only be earning $600 a month. Leila's bedroom was a cot set up in the basement beside the furnace. She prayed to the whirl of the machine and, in the damp winter months, shivered under her blankets. There was no door to her room, so the children could come and go as they pleased. Leila was also not allowed to use the computer to email or call her family except for Sunday mornings and only for one hour.

All the while, her employer said she was one of the family and should make herself feel comfortable. She had to eat on her own and she was not allowed to buy her own food. She knew no one except a few nannies she began meeting at the park when she took the four-year-old. She felt lonely and isolated. One day, some of the Filipina nannies Leila befriended at the park told her to speak to her employer about having one day off a week, if not two, and to reduce her hours so she could have evenings free to pray and knit, as she liked to make her children sweaters.

Leila got the courage to do so. Her employer was furious, wanting to know with whom she was speaking who would advise her so poorly. Her employer took her passport and said that, if she didn't do as she was told, Leila could return to the Philippines. She would put her back on the airplane, but there was no way she was staying in Canada unless she followed her rules. "I will have you deported!" she screamed at Leila.

Leila was heartbroken. When she finally had a chance to call her husband, she broke down crying. But she couldn't tell him the truth as to why. She was homesick and feeling like she made a big mistake. She told her husband, instead, that she just missed their children, but the job was going well. She didn't want him to worry about her.

Leila's employer gave her more work to do than ever. She would make lists of things to do during the day, including cleaning the silverware, dropping clothes off at the dry cleaner, cleaning the fridge and gardening. The family also had two dogs that Leila was now responsible for walking.

Then one day, Leila was in the kitchen and the four-year-old called her "yellow skin." Leila was trying to get him to eat some carrots. He threw them at Leila's face and hissed: "You're not my mom. You can't tell me what to do. Go home, yellow skin." The boy started wailing, alerting Leila's employer, who came running. When she saw the child upset, she got mad at Leila. When Leila recounted what the child had said to her, her employer slapped her across the face. "How dare you accuse my son of being bad! Go to your room."

Leila's employer started docking her salary whenever anything on her list was not completed. Leila felt shy and insecure around all the children. She walked with her head down and kept her gaze to the floor. The once happy and upbeat young woman fell into a deep depression. She feared for her physical safety as her employer had her passport. She was overworked and tired.

The other nannies at the park recognized that Leila was being bullied and got her to open up about the emotional blackmail going on at home. The training programs in the Philippines did not tell Leila she had legal rights in Canada, even under the Live-In Caregiver Program, including a locked room to sleep in, overtime pay and days off.

Leila feared coming forward and filing a complaint with Immigration because her employer had her passport and said she would have her deported should she disobey any order. The nannies said this was also against the law. Leila, nonetheless, was too afraid to do anything. All she could think about was the better life she was giving her children through her salary and their eventual residency in Canada.

But things turned worse. One night, her employer's husband came into the furnace room drunk and tried to attack Leila. She fended him off by throwing her bible at him. He was too drunk to protest and just passed out. The next day, however, her employer fired her, saying that she had come on to her husband and that she was a slut. Leila had an hour to pack her things and find somewhere to go. On the way out the door, her employer returned the passport.

Luckily, Leila had the other nannies, and they referred her to an agency in Vancouver that helps live-in caregivers in distress. Leila eventually found another job with a good employer who paid her fairly, didn't overwork her or threaten her with deportation. Leila discovered that most nannies in Canada are from the Philippines and that few know they have legal and human rights. Even if they do know, most are too afraid while under the program to file complaints against their employers.

The LCP is ripe with abuse, from physical harassment to emotional blackmail. Many have called it modern-day slavery, in which the workplace has moved from the business towers to the kitchens and living rooms, and many parents seem to take advantage of the power they have over these women from developing countries, desperate to earn incomes to support their families and provide better lives for their children. Leila was a broken woman after her first experience in Canada, and her story represents so many others.

Sadly, Leila and Canadian families are far from the only ones guilty of exploiting workers. It is a worldwide epidemic. Camilla Schick and the BBC recently reported on the plight of Thai farm workers in Israel. According to Human Rights Watch, 173 Thai workers on ten farming communities were low paid, worked excessive hours, lived in dangerous conditions and denied the right to change employers—all in defiance of Israel's labor laws. To add insult to injury, a recent law entitling them to tax credits means they are now paying full taxes on their paltry income.

These workers live in shared space in crowded huts, alongside the overwhelming stench of cow manure with little or no access to healthcare—with no ability to take time off for illness because they'll be docked pay. Between 2008 and 2013, one hundred and twenty-two Thai Nationals died on these farms. The causes include: accidents, alcohol poisoning, suffocation, suicide, beatings and heart failure; several simply died in their sleep. One worker said he worked thirteen-hour days, seven days a week, for three years. "People get so tired, their bodies cannot take it." This amounts to modern day slavery and needs to be addressed on a global scale immediately.

Bullying and Stakeholders External to the Organization

Stakeholders other than employees are not immune from being bullied.

There are numerous reported incidents:

- In policing, brutality seems routine.

- In nursing, patients being abused by healthcare providers and healthcare providers being bullied by patients and or the patient's family members.

- In education, teachers and professors seeking sexual favors in exchange for higher marks, and students and/or parents bullying teachers in retaliation for not progressing or receiving lower marks.

- In retail and the service industry, customers bullying sales people.

As with employees, it is difficult to capture the true dimensions of the problem because the targets and bystanders are afraid to report. In policing, the use of cameras to record interactions between officers and citizens they apprehend is proving to be an effective deterrent.

In Dictatorial and Disjointed cultures, particularly if there are no appropriate checks and balances, service providers and vendors are subject to bullying, usually under the rationalization that the buyer is just driving a hard bargain. In organizations that have lax ethical standards, bully buyers prosper.

Learning from the parents—Toni's story

Until June of 2009, Toni was a teacher at a private school for girls. Toni was an exceptionally good teacher and scored well in her performance reviews and student feedback in each of the five years she taught there. Prior to her posting at this school, Toni spent eleven years in the public school system. Toni also has a Master's of Education degree.

In January of 2009, the parents of one of Toni's seventh-grade students asked to meet with her. At the meeting, the parents expressed their displeasure at their daughter Julie's grades. Toni indicated to the parents that, while Julie definitely had the potential for higher grades, her attitude and lack of application were holding her back. Julie's parents reacted badly to this and indicated that they would take the matter up with Margaret, the school's head.

Julie's parents lodged a complaint that Toni graded Julie unfairly. They also indicated that Toni was rude when they met. Toni indicated that she was very fair in the grades she gave, in that there was little subjectivity. Margaret asked Toni to reassess, to which Toni responded that she would be happy to, conditional on Julie being retested in her low-scoring subjects. Margaret felt that this was appropriate and advised the parents, who did not like the idea, but agreed, provided that Julie be given three weeks to study for the exams. Toni observed that giving Julie this time to study for the retesting could have her fall behind in her current courses.

Three weeks later, Julie took the exams and the grading was marginally better, also, as Toni predicted, Julie fell behind in her current courses. The parents went back to Margaret and complained that Julie was set up for failure and that Toni made the re-examination tougher than the original tests. They also complained that Toni retaliated against Julie by being harder on her than other students and that this was why Julie was falling further behind. Margaret supported Toni by reminding them that Toni had warned that Julie might fall behind. She also indicated that, in the five years Toni taught there, no complaints had ever been lodged.

For the next few weeks, Margaret received at least one call a week from Julie's parents with complaints ranging from how Toni was treating Julie, ignoring her, to singling her out with the most difficult questions, making fun of her in front of other students and threatening to give her failing grades. Margaret went to Toni every time a complaint was made. Toni denied every allegation and asked Margaret to interview Julie and other students in the class. Margaret did this and found Julie to be very belligerent. When asked, other students responded to the question, "Does Ms. Allen single any students out for special treatment or punishment?" they felt that Toni treated everyone the same and made a point of telling Margaret how much they liked her. One of the students mentioned that Julie had told her "my parents are going to get Ms. Allen fired."

This validated for Margaret that Julie's parents were definitely out to get Toni. Margaret met with Richard, the long-standing chair of the board, about her concerns and asked him to intervene with Julie's parents. Richard indicated that he was uncomfortable doing this as the parents had already approached him and he felt that there was some merit to their concerns for Toni.

Margaret was dumbfounded and asked why he had not come to her. Richard indicated he had questions regarding how she (Margaret) handled the situation and wanted to consult with other board members before he approached her. "Well, I expect that you will do this before the week is finished, because if you don't, I will call a meeting with the entire board so that I can relay to them what is going on. You are obviously taking Julie's and her parents' word on this over mine and I do not have the confidence that you will properly represent and support Toni and me on this matter."

Surprised, Richard backtracked. indicating he had not formed a judgment, but wanted advice from others before he proceeded.

"Well, I don't understand why you didn't come to me first," Margaret responded, adding, "Toni is being bullied by Julie and her parents and I want it stopped; that's why I came to you." Richard and Margaret agreed to meet early the next week to determine a course of action.

At that meeting, Richard told Margaret that Julie's family had a long history with the school and the parents were major donors.

"I am well aware of this and I do not understand why that should have any bearing on the situation; it does not give them license to bully," Margaret interjected.

"Well, the board does not share your view; in fact, they agree with Julie's parents that Toni is the bully here," Richard replied.

Richard added that the board decided that Toni should be let go and directed Margaret to inform her. Margaret disagreed with this decision, and said, if the board did not reconsider, she would view this as a lack of confidence in her and a dismissal. Richard considered this insubordination and fired her.

Toni thanked Margaret for standing up for her and was distressed that Margaret lost her position because of it. Both

Margaret and Toni filed constructive dismissal suits and settled out of court for considerably more than they would have received under normal severance arrangements because the board did not want to have it made public.

A new head was recruited. Julie's new teacher was forced to fudge her grades. Richard and the board are still in place.

The customer is always right— Allen's story

Allen was a Sales Associate in the Women's department of a high-end department store chain. He joined them in January of 2010 after moving back to Toronto from New York City, where he spent eleven years with a similar high-end retailer.

In May of 2010, a customer, Ms. Jones, bought an evening gown from Allen. While Ms. Jones was in the customer database as a frequent shopper, this was the first time Allen sold to her.

After the sale, Nancy, another sales associate said to Allen, "I'll bet you a drink that she returns the dress on Monday."

Allen asked, "Why do you say that?"

"Oh, she does it all the time, here, and at other stores. When she has a fancy function to go to she 'buys' a garment, wears it to the event and returns it after, claiming either it is flawed, bad fit or she didn't like it after she got home."

Allen asked Nancy, "Why is she not flagged in the system?" Nancy indicated that the rumour was that Ms. Jones was well connected in the community and. if there were any trouble she had the ability to convince other customers to boycott the store.

Sure enough, the following Monday, Ms. Jones returned the gown, claiming that the color just was not right for her.

Allen said that he had to check with the manager, Nigel, who was very familiar with Ms. Jones and approved the credit. When Allen objected, Nigel said, "Don't fight it, kid, that's the way it is," adding, "Remember one thing, Allen, around here the customer is always right."

While giving Ms. Jones the credit, Allen asked her how she enjoyed the event on Saturday night. In a haughty tone, Ms. Jones asked, "What are you implying, young man?"

"Nothing really, my friends saw you there."

The next morning, Allen was called into Nigel's office and told that Ms. Jones had called the owner of the store to complain that Allen had been impertinent. Allen told Nigel what he said and observed that Ms. Jones obviously made the connection that he knew that she had worn the returned gown to the event. Nigel told Allen that the owner wanted Allen to send a note of apology with a $100 gift certificate (which would be deducted from his commission). Allen refused and was fired.

Allen filed for wrongful dismissal and the case proceeded to discovery. Allen did his homework and found ten instances where Ms. Jones had purchased evening gowns over a two-year period and made returns after she wore them to events. He also had pictures from the society pages, including the gown he had "sold" to her.

Allen's lawyer indicated to the store's lawyer that they intended on calling Ms. Jones as a witness. When the owner became aware of this, she instructed the lawyer to do whatever it took to settle. Allen received a handsome cash settlement and letters of apology from the owner and Ms. Jones (something that Allen insisted be part of the settlement).

How Big Is the Issue?

"Have you ever been bullied at work?"

To answer that all-important question, Ellen Cobb reported on the Monster Global Poll that tallied the responses of 16,517 workers worldwide in 2011:

"...64% answered that they had been bullied, either physically hurt, driven to tears, or had their work performance affected; 36% replied that this had never happened to them; and 16% answered that they had seen it happen to others. An astounding 83% of European respondents reported that they had been physically or emotionally bullied, while the percentages were 65% in the Americas, and 55% in Asia."

In November of 2012, Joanne Royce, in her blog, reported that 40 percent of Canadians are bullied at work. She cited Jacqueline Power, Assistant Professor of Management at the Odette School of Business, who has done extensive research on bullying in the workplace. According to Power, bullying is virtually never reported to management because, when people do report, "they don't get much support and Human Resource managers don't often respond to the allegations."

European research into the problem began in the early 1980s in Scandinavian countries and spread during the late 1990s to other European countries, Australia, New Zealand, and Asia.

It was through the work of Loraleigh Keashly (Wayne State University, Detroit, MI) in the 1990s, that a conceptual framework for workplace bullying emerged in the United States. Prior to this, there has been very little research in English on the topic.

According to a VitalSmarts study by David Maxfield and Joseph Grenny, 96 percent of respondents say they have experienced workplace bullying; 89 percent have suffered for more than a year and 54 percent have been under attack for more than five years. The study also addressed the three primary forms bullying takes:

1. Sabotaging others' work or reputations

2. Browbeating, threats or intimidation

3. Physical intimidation or assault

In most cases, between the bully and the victim, the bullies are most likely to retain their jobs. More than 60 percent of the victims either quit or are forced out; while only 15 percent of bullies suffer the same fate. Even though 51 percent of employees say their company has a policy for dealing with bullies, only 7 percent know of anyone who has ever used that policy.

Based on the research done to date it is reasonable to believe that the majority of employees, at some time during their career, will be exposed to systematic bullying or other forms of abusive behavior either directly or indirectly.

Costs, **Liabilities** and Deadly Consequences

"Workplace bullying–in any form–is bad for
business. It destroys teamwork, commitment and
morale."
–Tony Morgan, Chief Executive,
The Industrial Society

In *The Cost Of Bad Behavior: How Incivility is Damaging Your Business and What To Do About It*, Christine Porath, Ph.D., from Georgetown University indicated that time wasted at work or spent searching for another job could cost companies up to $300 billion a year. Further, the American Institute of Stress (AIS) estimates that one million workers are absent each workday in the US due to stress. The Institute calculated that it costs companies $300 billion a year in absenteeism, health expenses, and programs to help workers manage stress. This estimate does not include the cost of reduced productivity due to lowered morale, recruitment and training costs for new hires, stress-related workman's comp claims, bad press, or litigation.

In a poll of 800 managers and employees in seventeen industries, Christine Porath and her associate Christine Pearson found: "Among workers who've been on the receiving end of incivility:

- 48 percent intentionally decreased their work effort.

- 47 percent intentionally decreased the time spent at work.

- 38 percent intentionally decreased the quality of their work.

- 80 percent lost work time worrying about the incident.

- 63 percent lost work time avoiding the offender.

- 66 percent said that their performance declined.

- 78 percent said that their commitment to the organization declined.

- 12 percent said that they left their job because of the uncivil treatment

- 25 percent admitted to taking their frustrations out on customers."

Although difficult to calculate, brand and reputation value takes a major hit in instances where violence in the workplace is exposed in the media. Consider what Rutgers University is experiencing after the video exposing bullying exploded in the media.

And the costs are more than just financial.

Every year, nearly 2 million American workers report being victimized by workplace violence, ranging from sexual or physical assault to homicide. And almost 10 percent of workplace fatalities are homicides. While many more men die at work than women, of women who die while working, nearly a quarter of them are homicides; whereas, fewer than 10 percent of men who die at work are killed by someone else. Exacerbating the issue, according to a 2002 FBI report on workplace violence, the majority of incidents aren't reported to management, never mind the police, making it a larger problem than we can even quantify—or address successfully.

An example is Christopher Dorner, the former Los Angeles Police Department officer who is alleged to have killed four people and targeted as many as fifty other officers and their families in revenge for his 2008 firing. His act of terrorism ended in a barrage of bullets and a blazing fire in a cabin in California's San Bernardino Mountains on February 12, 2013. There is now an investigation in response to suggestions that Dorner was bullied by officers he targeted and blamed for his being fired.

A series of events in South Korea is drawing scrutiny by the government of Korea's Defense Ministry; one involved a bullied marine corporal who went on a shooting rampage killing four marines and wounding another, a number of suicides where bullying was a factor, a military culture of bullying and beating.

In September of 2009, Jim Badasci, who worked ten years at Fresno Equipment Company in California, went to work with a shotgun and killed a fellow coworker. Four others convinced him to stop shooting and, rather than killing them, Badasci killed himself. A fellow coworker said what Badasci did was out of character and told Mark Ames of the "eXile" website that Badasci had "been driven to desperation by a particular supervisor and the company's tolerance of the supervisor's mistreatment."

A documentary, *Murder By Proxy: How America Went Postal* gives a dramatic history of the increasing number of mass murders in the United States and how bullying in the workplace is a major factor.

Someone commits suicide every 15 minutes according to the Centers for Disease Control and Prevention. While there is very little research to date on specific links of suicides or attempted suicides due to workplace bullying, there can be little doubt that it is a contributing factor when we consider that bullying is one of the main contributing or substantive factors in the suicide of children and young adults.

On July 30, 2010, Kevin Morrissey, managing editor at the University of Virginia literacy magazine *Virginia Quarterly Review*, shot himself. Warnings and red flags to university officials by coworkers and Morrissey's sister went unheeded. It was reported that Morrissey placed at least eighteen calls to university officials in the final two weeks of his life.

In France, there is an ongoing criminal investigation into allegations that management practices at France Telecom, now Orange France, led several employees to commit suicide in recent years. The suicide rate at the telecommunications giant exceeds the national average. The probe is looking into a single case and will determine whether France Telecom and one of its managers could be brought to trial for involuntary homicide. This case has brought forward the probable connection between workplace bullying and suicide. In July of 2012, authorities placed the former head of France Telecom, Didier Lombard, under formal investigation. Lombard ultimately resigned because of it.

In March of 2014, Orange initiated another investigation in the suicides of ten employees since the beginning of the year. Most of the reasons were "explicitly related to their jobs."

In July of 2014, Michael Talbot and Avery Haines of Toronto's CTV broadcast a three-part investigation that reported the suicides of two Toronto police officers who suffered from Post Traumatic Stress Disorder. According to former Staff Sergeant Simon Fraser, more officers will die because of being bullied into keeping their PTSD hidden.

Workplace Bullying and Post Traumatic Stress Disorder (PTSD)

The German Psychotherapist Dr. Heinz Leymann found that people who had been relentlessly bullied at work suffered more intense and persistent Post Traumatic Stress Disorder (PTSD) than train conductors who witnessed suicides by people throwing themselves in front of the train. He discovered that PTSD is probably the correct psychiatric and psychological diagnosis for an astounding 95 percent of the targets of bullying. In an article in the *European Journal of Work and Organizational Psychology*, Dr. Leymann and Annelie Gustafsson found the train operators' symptoms to be "very much milder" than all of the targets in their workplace bullying study. In fact, the authors found that the reactions of targets of bullying compare more closely with a Norwegian study concerning raped women.

The core elements of PTSD include captivity or entrapment, psychological fragmentation, the loss of a sense of safety, trust, and self worth, as well as the tendency to be re-victimized. It is not difficult to see how these elements are at play in the workplace. There is certainly a sense of captivity or entrapment because people are usually dependent on their employment for their livelihood. Many adults spend more time at work than they do with their families, or sleeping, so it is understandable that the psychological impact of being bullied includes the loss of a sense of safety, trust and self worth. Typically, workplace bullying is repeated and ongoing, so it stands to reason that the target feels re-victimized, because they are being retargeted. And if the organization handles the situation poorly, they will once again be retargeted.

Leymann points out that the train drivers did not experience an ongoing series of trauma or identity insults from different societal sources as the raped women and bullied employees did. "Mobbing [bullying] and expulsion from the labor market are in themselves a series of victimizations of traumatic strength . . . torn out of their social network, a life of early retirement with permanent psychological damage threatens the great majority of mobbing victims."

They found that many of the targets of bullying experienced mental effects fully comparable with PTSD from war or prison camp experiences.

A number of serious health conditions, both psychological and physical, can accompany PTSD:

- "depression

- obsession

- agitation

- blockage of the memory of the events

- a resigned attitude

- moderate cognitive disturbances

- automatically recurring thoughts

- irritability

- inner unrest

- panic/anxiety attacks

- hyposomnia

- addiction

- suicidal ideation, thoughts, plans, and attempts

- gastro-intestinal disturbances

- muscular disorders

- chronic muscle hypertension."

Given these symptoms, it is no small wonder that the performance of targeted people deteriorates and they are viewed as being insubordinate and having a poor attitude. They suffer the symptoms of PTSD; they give the bully the ammunition for continued bullying.

While there are presently no quantitative studies measuring the relationship between divorce and PTSD as a result of bullying, from the abundant anecdotal data available, it is clear that marital breakdown is often one of the casualties. Thus, the target is even more alone with even less of a support structure, and carries the guilt and hurt.

CASE STUDY

A father's confession—Tim's story

In 2010, Tim's dad, Fred, called him to come to his place as soon as possible. "I don't have much time left and I have a confession to make before I go," was his somber plea.

At twenty-five, Tim was the eldest of Fred's three children. Fred left his wife Mary eight years prior and lived with his elderly mother, who was the only person who would have him. Fred was an unemployed alcoholic and he had very little contact with his family since he left. Tim recalls Fred's drinking problem started around ten years earlier, when Tim was fifteen, and suspected that it was related to Fred being fired from his position as CFO of a Canadian retailer in 1998. In the few years before he left, Fred was verbally and physically abusive to everyone in the family.

While Tim was civil whenever he had contact with Fred, he resented him for leaving and he considered Fred a loser. Andrea and Jim, Tim's brother and sister, were more charitable in their feelings towards Fred, as was Mary. She regularly sent Fred's mother a check to help her with expenses, as she knew Fred had no income and her mother-in-law was not in a financial position to support him.

Fred was in a lot of pain; Tim could tell when they met. Fred told Tim the whole story and, by the time he was finished, Tim felt both outrage and regret. Outrage for what happened to his dad and regret on how he treated and misjudged him.

Fred joined his company in 1987 as comptroller and was promoted to CFO in 1996, reporting to Janice the CEO. Janice was a very demanding boss, but because of his performance and capabilities, Fred did not suffer the abuse Janice regularly doled out to others in the organization.

In August of 1997, Fred was offered a CFO position with a larger retailer. When he told Janice he was leaving, she begged him to reconsider, giving him a huge raise, a staying bonus and a promise that he would be considered as her replacement in a few years' time. Fred reconsidered and decided to stay.

In about a month, Janice started to ride Fred, criticizing almost everything he did. The emails from Janice were endless, every day, at all hours, weekends and holidays. Janice expected immediate responses, and if he did not, she would send another email. Janice started excluding Fred from critical meetings, did not communicate decisions she made and started dealing directly with one of Fred's subordinates without involving him.

This eroded Fred's confidence and, as a result, his performance. He did not know how to handle the situation. This is when he started to drink heavily, which led to the downward spiral. Because of the stress and the drinking, Fred gained weight and started having heart problems.

The harassment and abuse lasted eleven months. In August of 1999, exactly a year after Fred told Janice he was leaving, Janice fired Fred "for cause," citing his poor performance over the last year. Her parting comment was, "Nobody quits on me!"

Fred sought legal advice and the lawyer indicated to him that Janice had built up a very good case for terminating him and advised him to accept the three months severance that Janice offered. Feeling he had no choice, Fred accepted the offer. Totally broken, unfit, and an alcoholic, Fred was not able to find new employment. Janice blacklisted Fred by discrediting him in the industry.

Having told Tim, Fred felt great relief. It was the first time he had confided to anyone about what he had gone through because he was ashamed. His health deteriorated to the point that he had only weeks to live and he wanted to make things right and apologize to his family, and he chose Tim as the conduit.

AUTHOR'S NOTE—Fred passed away five weeks later. Believing he was at fault rather than the victim was the major reason for his downfall, which happens with all too many targets. There is no question that Fred suffered from PTSD, and if he had not been alone to deal with what he went through, or those who were close to him recognized the symptoms and intervened, Fred might be alive today.

I can clearly relate to what Fred went through as I was bullied and retaliated against because I blew the whistle and exposed a corrupt executive. While I am unable to relate my story–in my case, I am bound by a nondisclosure agreement–I am able to tell the stories of others like Fred who have been negatively affected because of bullying in the work place.

For me, the experience was physically and emotionally debilitating. Also, for too long, I was made to believe that I was the culprit; my self-confidence was destroyed and my relationship with family, friends, and associates was severely tested. I fell into what I call the bully's trap, which, I have discovered, is all too common with people who are targeted.

Part Three:
Effectively Dealing with
the Issue

"Knowing what's right doesn't mean much unless
you do what's right."
–THEODORE ROOSEVELT

The Barriers

Bullying cannot be stopped by the ineffective techniques commonly used by Human Resource people. Sensitivity and diversity training, conflict resolution techniques and sending the bully to charm school do not work.

There are five main obstacles to stopping bullying:

1. Fear. Bullying is rarely reported by either the bullied or the bystander.

- Those who do report are usually labeled "disgruntled employees" or "troublemakers," and are discredited and retaliated against.

- Those who leave the organization because of bullying and/or whistleblowing often find they are blacklisted and have difficulty finding alternate employment.

2. Awareness and Concern

- Awareness. Like a bully's targets, bystanders may be unaware that what they are observing is bullying. Even if they can identify the actions and behaviors as bullying, they may not be aware of what they can do to help the target.

- Concern. Lack of concern on the part of bystanders is a difficult problem. This may be because of their own insensitivity or callousness, or it could be because they have sided with the bully and/or feel it in their best interest to protect themselves rather than the person being targeted. Also, if the target goes down, they may benefit.

3. The Attitudes and Behaviors of Leaders

- The CEO is also the CBO (Chief Bullying Officer)— Bosses are the bullies in over 70 percent of the reported incidents.

- Leaders who do not view verbal or psychological abuse as violence or do not make the connection that predatory aggression can give rise to physical aggression.

- Leaders who like bullies because they believe bullies get things done and are high performers.

- Leaders who think employees will abuse workplace violence/harassment legislation, policies and procedures. They fear that any intervention will be considered harassment. In 2010, Michael Bloomberg, the former Mayor of New York City, warned that if the State of New York passed proposed legislation, many companies would move their work to New Jersey. He effectively said: "If we don't allow companies to abuse employees, they won't be competitive!"

4. Organizational Response

- Ignore the problem or retaliate against the target. In the majority of cases where abuse is reported, the employer ignores the problem or makes the problem worse by retaliating against the target.

- Label a bullying situation as a personality clash, or an aggressive management style.

- Apply conflict resolution techniques, which makes the situation worse for the target.

5. Governance

- Boards of Directors that do not monitor or audit cultural factors of an organization or have appropriate checks and balances in place to predict and identify bullying.

Many jurisdictions have workplace violence and/or harassment legislation. Where there is legislation, only about 30 percent comply. Some organizations that put policies, procedures and programs in place do so just to be legally compliant, not necessarily to stop the bullying. Workplace bullying and serious organizational problems go hand in hand.

In my experience, where bullying occurs, the following dynamics are usually at play:

- Leaders score very low on the respectability scale.

- Fear is used as a substitute for motivation and positive leadership.

- There is a disproportionate focus on the short term, at the expense of sustainable long-term performance.

- Leaders do not appreciate the risks to brand and reputation when bullying is exposed.

- Leaders condone lax ethical standards.

- People are considered expendable.

- Performance management and advancement are ambiguous and/or subjective.

- Individual performance is rewarded over team performance.

- There are few checks and balances.

- Contrary viewpoints or opinions are not welcome.

- The governance level is negligent.

As I asserted in Part One, workplace bullying is part of a larger systemic issue that requires systemic change. For bullying to stop, a cultural change that is culturally and organizationally centered is required.

Importantly, it's also expensive. Workplace stress is an important economic issue. The American Institute of Workplace Stress estimates that companies lose $300 billion per year in absenteeism, health expenses, and stress management programs. That figure doesn't include the billions more from reduced productivity and morale, recruitment and training costs for new hires, compensation claims, and litigation.

Bullying and the Attraction and Retention of Talent

Attraction and retention of talent will become the biggest catalyst for organizations to ensure that their workplaces are safe and free from bullying.

I have worked with a number of companies in a variety of sectors across North America on cultural transformation. For many, what triggered the initiative was the ability to attract and retain talent. Many wanted to build on cultures to establish themselves as the organization of choice, for both customers and employees. One bank I worked with decided establishing the firm as the firm of choice for women with wealth and women in wealth as their Number One initiative.

Within five years, attracting and retaining talent will emerge as the biggest challenge for employers. This is already the case in some sectors, including health care and technology.

Notwithstanding current levels of unemployment, demographics dictate that the number of people available to work will decrease at a greater rate than the demand for employees in most sectors and categories of employees.

In addition to a declining work force, research shows that employees will defect at increasing rates. A 2010 survey of British workers indicates that an astounding 50 percent want to leave their current organization when the economy is strong. The main reason: conflict with their boss or coworker (read: bully-ing). Realistically, not all of the 50 percent are going to defect, but the extent of the discontent is disturbing.

One organization I worked with had great difficulty convinc-ing search firms to recruit for them because the organization had a terrible reputation, where bullying was not only condoned, but encouraged.

As part of the cultural transformation process, I encourage organizations to develop a Value Exchange Model (based on the Ethics of Reciprocity) for the various employee categories. In retail, the Value Exchange Model for customers is widely used by Tier One retailers. This model outlines the importance of understanding and delivering on the expectations that each have of the other.

A fairly recent, but growing factor in this conversation is the migration to "temp" or "gig" work: contract workers who are, by definition short-term. In the past ten years alone, nearly ten million additional workers became contractors as their primary profession.

In addition to absorbing the cost of healthcare, time off and pensions, these workers are particularly vulnerable to bullying as they are always looking for the next contract: they can't afford to make waves because they are the first to be let go and risk future work.

Corporations should note that the risk is not all on their con-tract workers. Employers also lose talent, decrease cooperation and collaboration in the workplace and are less likely to invest in training and development, which, ultimately, weakens the value of their workforce.

Factoring Bullying into the Being Hired/ Hiring Equation

Given that there may be choices for people when they decide to change employment, the cultures of prospective employers will become a major factor.

In making the decision to change employers, I encourage people to conduct thorough due diligence and avoid going from a known situation to one that is unknown and potentially toxic. In "Pam's Story—Onto Pleasure Island," I relay what happened to Pam when she left a positive situation after nine successful years and found herself in a totally toxic one. Had Pam done better due diligence, she could have avoided what became a living nightmare that continues to haunt her.

When considering a change, I recommend the following:

1. Understand what you are leaving.

For more than 70 percent of those who are bullied, the only way to stop the bullying is to quit. You do not have to quit to have the bullying stop and, if this is the main or only reason, you should consider your options.

2. Have the search firm/recruiter consider you an equal client.

The search firm/recruiter has inside knowledge of the organization and should be able to answer questions regarding the culture and history of the organization and its people.

While the organization is the paying client, potential and successful candidates must be considered equally as clients. Part of what the search firm must do is properly and honestly make people aware of what they are getting into and be held accountable if they misrepresent the situation and, as in Pam's case, if it does not work out, provide the ability to seek legal recourse.

3. Find out as much as you can about the organization.

- Talk to people you know in the organization. If you don't know anyone, as part of the recruitment process, ask to have access to two or three people who will give candid input. Being able to speak to the person you are replacing will provide valuable insight. If you know former employees of the organization, they will likely be more comfortable being candid.

- Check the Internet for any media reports related to bullying/violence, sexual harassment, human rights claims, class action lawsuits, reported or alleged wrongdoings, and union certification drives.

- Talk to people external to the organization. Vendors and clients you may know will have insights and viewpoints that can help you assess.

4. Questions you should ask.

- What are the values and operating principles, and how are they applied?

- What are the characteristics of the culture in the organization? (See section "What's Culture Got to Do with It.")

- Who am I replacing? And if that person left, how long was s/he with the organization and in the position and why did s/he leave?

- What is the turnover rate in the organization and the department?

- Are exit interviews conducted? What are the reasons people cited for leaving?

- Why is this an external hire?

- As part of the hiring and advancement to management processes, are psychological assessments conducted? (If the answer to this one is no—beware!)

- What is the investment in management and leadership training?

- Do regions and/or departments operate on an integrated basis or as silos?

- Describe the performance management system. What gets measured? What's the balance between individual and team? To what extent are performance reviews two-way discussions?

- Do terms of engagement exist for resolving differences and disputes?

- Are there policies, procedures and practices in place relating to codes of conduct and conflict of interest?

- What are the highlights of the latest employee attitude/engagement survey? What was the participation rate in the latest survey?

- Is employee absenteeism a problem?

- What did the organization do to minimize negative impact on people during the economic downturn?

- Are contrarian viewpoints welcome?

- In terms of organizational priorities, where does talent rank? In the annual plan, what are the specific initiatives in place that focus on talent as a priority?

5. Find out as much as you can about the person you will be reporting to.

- Tenure with the organization and in the position
- Style
- Personality
- Any history of harassment or bullying
- Relationship with people in the department
- Relationship with the person you are replacing

In assessing the organization's culture, try to connect all of the information and look for inconsistencies. If there are inconsistencies, seek clarification.

6. Be honest about why you are making the change.

You will be asked why you are making a change. If the reason you are leaving your current employer is to stop the bullying, you don't have to get into the gory details. You can simply state that your values do not align with those of the organization.

Attraction and retention of talent should be one of the top priorities in every organization. The culture of the organization, or put another way, what the organization stands for and how it operates, is the biggest factor in why people decide to join and stay.

In the event you run into resistance, receive vague responses, or there are inconsistencies in the responses, consider them indicators of the culture that exists. The recruiter, in enticing you to join, will try to sell and, understandably, accentuate the positive. If you are informed, you will be able to determine if what is portrayed is real or not.

I also advise you to take notes of all of the conversations you have during the hiring process. This record will help you seek recourse if there has been a misrepresentation and the move ends badly.

Is There a Psychopath in the House?

As with most issues, there is rarely a magic bullet to resolve the problem. Bullying in the workplace is no exception. As I have previously stated, stopping bullying takes a comprehensive, integrated approach. There is one thing, however, that comes close to being a magic bullet: organizations making psychological testing mandatory for anyone being hired or promoted to a management or supervisory position.

A highly regarded psychologist, Robert Hare, developed a checklist of twenty telltale signs that help detect whether someone is a psychopath, which is defined in the *Diagnostic and Statistical Manual of Mental Disorders* as Antisocial Personality Disorder and characterized by individuals who habitually violate the rights of others without remorse. This description matches many of the bullies that I have profiled. Hare is convinced many important CEOs and politicians fall into this category.

Dean Haycock, Ph.D, summarized the twenty telltale signs developed by Hare as follows:

- "glib and superficial charm

- grandiose (exaggeratedly high) estimation of self

- need for stimulation

- pathological lying

- cunning and manipulative

- lack of remorse or guilt

- shallow affect (superficial emotional responsiveness)

- callousness and lack of empathy

- parasitic lifestyle

- poor behavioral controls

- sexual promiscuity

- early behavioral problems

- lack of realistic long-term goals

- impulsiveness

- failure to accept responsibility for one's own actions

- many short-term marital relationships

- juvenile delinquency

- revocation of conditional release

- criminal versatility."

Organizations should rely on professionals such as industrial psychologists to make the assessments.

I flunked the test and they still hired me!—Andrew's story

One company, a conglomerate of a number of related business units I worked with, has had psychological assessment as part of its hiring and advancement protocol for more than two decades. This company had the characteristics of a Stable culture. The CEO decided to retire after a very successful twelve-year run. The board selection committee established the criteria for the new CEO and they placed a heavy emphasis on bringing in a change agent: someone who had the experience and background to reinvent the company. While the company was very successful in the past, market conditions and new competition threatened the sustainability of revenue and earnings growth.

After an extensive and long international search process, the search committee identified an individual who looked like a perfect match to the profile established. On paper, Andrew was by far the most qualified of any of the other candidates. He interviewed well and he was a recognized change agent having turned around three major organizations in the last fifteen years. As is the case when attracting someone away from another organization, it was difficult to obtain direct references. Those that the executive recruiter was able to get were positive, particularly regarding Andrew's background and experience. One common theme, however, was that Andrew was very demanding and "does not suffer fools lightly."

When Andrew was told that he had to go through a psychological assessment before an offer was made, he indicated that he viewed this as insulting and threatened to withdraw from the running. The executive recruiter, after much persuasion, convinced Andrew to have the assessment done, indicating to him that this was a long-standing protocol, and there were no exemptions. Andrew was also told not to worry about it, it was just a process that the head of Human Resources insisted on, and the selection committee had already made up their mind, regardless of the results of the assessment.

John, an industrial psychologist, had tested and interviewed candidates for management positions with the company for seven years, and had an incredible track record. The company only hired or promoted people who John felt would be successful in the culture. The management team were considered to be the best and the brightest in the industry. Turnover of staff was very low. On the annual engagement surveys, the scores for leadership, communication and being treated with respect were always higher than the benchmark of other companies. The performance and productivity metrics over the previous ten years exceeded those of benchmark companies in the industry, worldwide.

When John administered the test and interviewed Andrew, he knew almost from the outset that Andrew would not be a good fit. While Andrew was obviously on his best behavior during the interviews, with John he was defensive, mocked the process and declared, "When I become the CEO, you won't be doing much work with us." The assessment concluded that Andrew was close to being a psychopath.

John presented his findings to the head of Human Resources, the chair of the selection committee and the executive recruiter. Both the executive recruiter and the head of the selection committee rejected John's assessment. The executive recruiter discredited John referencing his reputation in the industry for not being objective, who did not like people who were demanding and tough. The head of Human Resources argued that John's track record was solid. The chair of the selection committee argued that the criteria they had established called for a change agent and "to make

the changes that need to be done, we need one tough bastard." At the insistence of the head of Human Resources,
John's report was submitted to the selection committee and
then to the full board.

The board was clearly divided. Most felt uncomfortable
in making an offer given the report. However, the head of
the selection committee made a strong argument citing the
need for "one tough bastard," and he also reminded them
that there was no strong alternative and that the board was
under tremendous pressure from shareholders to name a
CEO. After much debate, the decision was made to make
an offer to Andrew, which he accepted. No reference to the
assessment was made.

What John outlined in his report proved to be accurate.
According to the head of Human Resources, Andrew's
behavior was far worse than what he anticipated, knowing
what was in the report. Within one year from Andrew's date
of hire, the culture went from Stable to Dictatorial. Eight
of the twelve members of the senior management team
resigned, including the head of Human Resources.

Andrew brought in people (all male) who worked for him
at his previous companies to replace those who left. They
became Andrew's henchmen. Relationships with employees
and vendors deteriorated. Fault lines were starting to show;
all of the performance metrics were on a downward trend.
Andrew tried to force the CFO to report inflated revenue
and profit numbers. The CFO refused and Andrew fired her
for insubordination. She was given a huge severance with
the understanding that she would not reveal to anyone the
events surrounding her termination. The board was clueless
as to what was going on.

Two years into his tenure, Andrew knew that he could
only hide the inevitable for so long, so he decided that rather
than reinvent the company and grow it, the better option
was to divest any part that was not core. The board bought

into this strategy and 80 percent of the business was sold for a multiple much lower than its potential. The board considered Andrew a hero for avoiding what they thought was a potential long-term disaster, and gave him a multimillion-dollar incentive for successfully dismantling the company. Andrew also triggered the "change of control" provision in his agreement (which stipulated that if over 50 percent of the company were sold, a multimillion-dollar severance would be paid).

All of the businesses that were sold turned into great acquisitions and solid performers, validating what those in the know had suggested—that they were sold at too low a multiple.

AUTHOR'S NOTE—Andrew went on to become CEO of another major organization whose performance started to significantly deteriorate a year and a half after Andrew became its "leader."

The decline and fall of this company could have been avoided had the board taken the psychological assessment seriously.

Again, more than 70 percent of bullying is boss to subordinate. Not hiring or promoting a bully to a position of power reduces the risk of bullying. Having a scientifically proven method to identify bullies is close to a magic bullet to stop bullying from occurring, and I highly recommend that all organizations make a psychological assessment part of their management hiring and promotion protocol.

Part Four:

Guidance and Advice

"Never give in. Never give in. Never, never, never, never–in nothing, great or small, large or petty– never given in, except to convictions of honour and good sense. Never yield to force. Never yield to the apparently overwhelming might of the enemy."
–Winston Churchill

Overcoming It—Advice to the Bullied

"Although the world is full of suffering,
it is full also of the overcoming of it."
−HELEN KELLER

In most cases of bullying in the workplace, people allow it to happen, do not report it and try to deal with it on their own. Research shows that for more than 70 percent of those who are bullied, the only way for the bullying to stop is to quit. When this happens, the bully has clearly won and will very likely find a new target.

People react to bullying in different ways. Some just let it happen, others get angry and retaliate, some become bullies and take out their anger on others (often their families), and others revert to extreme measures such as seriously injuring or killing the people they feel are responsible for their being bullied and, for others, the only way out is to commit (or attempt) suicide.

It is my belief that people who are being bullied can respond in a positive and safe way, which, for them, will have a positive outcome.

There is no set formula or step-by-step process. What I offer is a number of points that should be used as a guide. Also, the approach should vary based on the organizational culture. For example, in a "Stable" culture, I encourage people to follow the process prescribed by the organization because there, the officials, usually Human Resources, can be trusted to act in the best interest of the person being bullied.

Conversely, in a "Dictatorial" culture, I recommend that people deal with their situation outside the process prescribed by the organization, because the officials, again, usually Human Resources, should be viewed with skepticism, as they either have zero influence to stop the bullying or they are part of the problem.

In what I describe as a "Disjointed" culture, I advise caution on whether to follow the process prescribed by the organization, and suggest only going to an internal official that one absolutely trusts.

Much can be learned from the experiences of others. Bullying is not a one-off situation. Bullying in an organization or by an individual usually follows a pattern. People are usually aware of others who have been bullied. Reaching out to them and having them relate their experiences will provide valuable insight on what to do, what to avoid, and who to trust.

If you are being bullied, I offer the following on what to do (and what not do).

1. Don't deal with it alone.

> "Trouble is part of your life—if you don't share it,
> you don't give the person who loves you a chance
> to love you enough."
> –DINAH SHORE

Talk to someone who is close to you about it. This is not something you should be ashamed of. You are not the first or only person dealing with it. It is not your fault. People you are close to want to—and can—help you through this. You need someone to think through the steps with you, challenge you, and help you develop a strategy.

Don't hide the situation from your family; they need to know, as they can also be victims, indirectly. Also, they will know something is wrong and will observe things about you that you may not be aware of: e.g., mood swings, disengagement, irritability, and if they are aware of what you are going through, they can not only help you through it, they can help you build your sense of self, which I believe is a prerequisite for taking an assertive position.

2. Build your "Sense of Self."

> "No one can make you feel inferior without your
> consent."
> –ELEANOR ROOSEVELT

Accept the fact that the bully wants to break you. Don't succumb to it! If you are being bullied at work, it takes over your life, it becomes your life, and it will undermine your sense of self.

Understand who you are and what you offer, at home, in your community, and at work. Many people withdraw when they are bullied. Do the opposite: become a better spouse, parent, son, daughter, friend, coach, mentor, volunteer, expert and producer. Feeling good about who you are, what you do, and what you offer will help you avoid the bullying from taking over your life. Exercise and the right diet are helpful in building on your sense of self when you go through this trauma.

Having this strong sense of self will also put you in a better frame of mind to deal with the bullying.

3. Don't become a bully who is targeted by another bully.

A bully who is targeted by another bully is both a target and a bully. In what I call a "Dictatorial culture," the CEO is usually a CBO who bullies his direct reports, who in turn bully the front line managers, who in turn bully the front line employees.

Dictatorial and Disjointed cultures are usually full of bullies who are targeted by other bullies. Often, in these cultures, people feel it is the only way to survive. They feel forced to behave in a manner that is inconsistent with their values and beliefs. Regardless of the culture in your organization, you can, not only survive, you can excel by staying true to your values and beliefs and treating people with respect and dignity. By doing this, you will garner the respect, loyalty and support of your peers and subordinates. Also, by doing this, you will be a role model for others who are being bullied. From my perspective, there is no better way to build on your sense of self than to be above it all and not allow yourself to act and behave inconsistently with your value system.

Reacting this way to being bullied is the most respectful form of revolt, and one that even the most powerful of bullies will have difficulty discrediting. As Mark Twain wrote, "Fewer things are harder to put up with than the annoyance of a good example."

4. Validate the bullying.

> "The man who is swimming against the stream
> knows the strength of it."
> —WOODROW WILSON

Organizations have the right to discipline, demote and fire. As outlined earlier, there are many ways and means of bullying.

You may be discriminated against, but that does not necessarily constitute bullying. You may be teased, but that does not necessarily mean you are being bullied. You may be confronted, someone may flirt with you, you may be subject to an incident of impulsive aggression, but again, these acts do not necessarily constitute bullying. Understanding what bullying is and what it is not and making distinctions (see "Making Distinctions") will help validate whether it's bullying.

Validating in your own mind that bullying is occurring will put you on the offense rather than the defense when you decide to confront the situation. Bullies, when confronted, usually will say things such as: "You are taking it the wrong way," "I don't mean to harm," "I'm passionate about the company and sometimes get carried away because of my passion," and "That's my style, and I am only doing what is expected of me to improve performance."

You must be ready for these pat answers by saying things like, "I understand, but these actions and behaviors constitute bullying."

Bullying is usually not one act. Bullies can be very subtle and manipulative and use various combinations of bullying. It is, therefore, important to relate seemingly unrelated comments, events and situations to fully outline and put into context what is happening to you.

5. Understand what motivates the bullying.

As indicated earlier, the primary reasons employees are targeted are:

- Retaliation

- Bigotry

- Exploitation

- Abuse of power

- To eliminate a threat

Knowing why you are being targeted will help you challenge the situation. Again, being able to assert or indicate that you strongly believe that you are being targeted will put you on the offense rather than on the defense. You are not likely the first or only target, and as such, whoever is dealing with the situation will not be able to ignore your assertion or belief. This, combined with the actions and behaviors of the bully, gives you credibility, particularly if it's possible to relate it to other similar situations.

6. Keep a detailed diary of what you are going through.

By documenting every comment, situation and event, you will be better able to, not only fully analyze what you are going through, but you will be better able to make your case. Bullies discredit their targets. By having the facts, properly framed and marshaled, you will be able to turn the situation around by discrediting the bully. For obvious reasons, bullies do not keep a running record of their actions and behaviors.

Bullies need to know that they will be held accountable for "creating unfavorable impressions" that are not true.

Record conversations you have with the bully. Small recorders that look like a pen are available at most electronic stores (some with video cameras are also available). Proof of these conversations detailing abusive or threatening language will add credibility to your position. The bully may claim that recording the conversation is illegal; you may counter that the bully's behavior is the illegal action. It is not illegal to record a conversation as long as one of the parties is aware. You are one of the parties.

7. Don't fall into the bully's trap.

"I learned long ago never to wrestle with a pig.
You get dirty, and besides, the pig likes it."
—GEORGE BERNARD SHAW

As I indicated earlier, bullies try to discredit their targets. The usual criticisms they lodge include deteriorating performance, poor attitude, insubordination and, ironically enough, poor people skills. While bullies don't document their actions and behaviors, rest assured they would document yours to build a case against you. My advice is: don't fall into this trap.

I know it will not be easy, but, rather than allow being bullied affect your performance or attitude, focus on excelling, keep your anger in check, and don't get sucked into a confrontation with the bully.

8. Don't get set up.

There are different ways and means of bullying. Bullies use tactics such as excluding you from essential meetings, giving you the wrong time for meetings to start, having you prepare for a topic different than what will be addressed, setting unreasonable expectations, and measuring your performance based on subjectivity and ambiguity. Having clarity around meetings, timing of meetings, agendas, expectations, and what you are measured on will help you avoid being set up.

Be assertive; have everything confirmed in writing. If you are not invited to a meeting that you should be, go to the meeting anyway. If you are not receiving correspondence or reports that you should be, figure out a way to get them. The message here is to be sensitive to everything that is going on and be one or two steps ahead of the bully.

9. Call the bully on it.

Timing is key here. Ideally, the first step is to simply indicate to the bully that you do not appreciate being bullied and ask that it be stopped. Do it in a respectful manner. Don't get into a debate. Just indicate that you know that you are being bullied and want it to stop. Bullies are not used to being called on their actions and behaviors. This direct request could possibly disarm him or her and stop the bullying.

If the bully wants to debate the issue, indicate that you are happy to do so, but you want a witness present. The witness should either be the bully's immediate superior or a Human Resource representative. Having a detailed diary of the comments, events and situations helps you control the situation.

At this session, do not accept rationalizations. Also, don't accept a conflict resolution approach, because this suggests that you are in a fight with the bully. Bullying is not a fight; it takes two or more to fight. Bullying is one-sided and you are on the receiving end. The purpose of the session is to register your expectation that the bullying stop. You should also put him or her on notice that if the bullying does not stop, and/or you are retaliated against because you made this request, you will take further steps.

If the bullying persists, and/or you are being retaliated against, register your complaint with someone in the organization you absolutely trust. In a Stable culture, it should be the head of Human Resources, in a Dictatorial or Disjointed culture, it could be the person in charge of legal or internal auditing.

"A fox should not be on the jury at a goose's trial."

–THOMAS FULLER

If the organization initiates an investigation, make sure you sign off on how the investigation will be conducted and who will be interviewed. You should be assured that the investigation would not become a "kangaroo court," where a disproportionate focus of the investigation is on you. In the section "Human Resources—Part of the Problem or Part of the Solution," I provide advice to human resource people on conducting investigations involving bullying.

10. Get professional help.

If you believe that you are being set up to be fired or you have lost control of the situation, seek advice from an employment lawyer or, if you are represented by a union, your union representative. Armed with your detailed diary, you will receive professional advice on what your legal options are. Courts are becoming less tolerant of employers who condone and/or encourage bullying. Remember, if you have your facts properly framed and marshaled, you are in a better position to take, or regain, control of the situation

Research shows that most of the people who are bullied suffer from Post Traumatic Stress Disorder (PTSD). The stress of being bullied can, and does, affect your physical and mental health. In some cases, it can lead people to take drastic action, the most extreme being murder and suicide. As I've said before, if you are having symptoms, don't deal with them alone: seek medical help. Remember, there should be no shame in what you are going through: it is not your fault. If you don't properly deal with the symptoms, you will allow the situation to control you and it could lead to an extremely bad outcome.

11. Help start the revolution for change.

"A good indignation brings out all one's powers."
—RALPH WALDO EMERSON

You, as a bullied employee, are also very likely a bystander, particularly if you work in a Dictatorial or Disjointed culture. When you control or stop the situation, you are in a powerful position to change it. While I have cautioned against anger, I encourage indignation. And this indignation over what you experienced should also carry over to what others in the organization go through.

"Let us not look back in anger, nor forward in fear,
but around in awareness."
—JAMES THURBER

Defining the Unjust—
Advice to the Bystander

"First they came for the communists, and I didn't
speak out because I wasn't a communist.
Then they came for the trade unionists, and I didn't
speak out because I wasn't a trade unionist.
Then they came for the Jews, and I didn't speak out
because I wasn't a Jew. Then they came for me and
there was no one left to speak for me."
–MARTIN NIEMOLLER

In the course of your working career, you will very likely be exposed to bullying and be a bystander. When this happens, you have to make choices: do nothing, actively or passively support the bully, or become a witness and/or defender, and/or a resister.

Choosing to be a witness, a defender or a resister is not free of risk; it requires courage. Choosing not to be a witness, defender, or resistor is also not free of risk when you consider:

- Could I have helped avoid a physical or mental breakdown?

- Could I have helped avoid ruining a career?

- Could I have helped avoid a family breakdown?

- Could I have helped avoid the organization's downfall?

- Could I have helped avoid a suicide (or attempted suicide)?

- Could I have helped avoid a murder?

All of these are real risks that I believe outweigh the risk of being a witness, defender and resister.

How you choose to handle the situation can help minimize the risk to you and the target. Do not be impulsive or reckless. You must be fact-based. Handle the situation with great sensitivity, tact and respect.

I offer the following advice on how you can help or try to help the target:

1. Become a witness.

When you either observe bullying or suspect that someone is being bullied, start taking notes of what you hear and see.

Even though the bullying may be subtle, there are lots of indicators. The main indicators are how the target reacts to the bullying. (Change in personality, withdrawn, disengaged, lashing out, slippage in performance, higher absenteeism, signs of substance abuse, negative comments about the organization and management, and other behaviors or comments that are uncharacteristic.)

The other indicators include comments made by other bystanders, the water cooler chitchat, gossip, comments made by the bully (remember, the bully is intent on discrediting the target), and the target being excluded from situations and correspondence. As this is likely not the bully's first target, comparing previous situations to this one can reveal other indicators.

Like those who are bullied, have facts properly framed and marshaled, register the existence of bullying, and your evidence will carry a lot of weight. Remember, bullies are unlikely to keep a running record of their actions and behaviors.

2. Validate the bullying.

We have outlined what constitutes bullying and what doesn't.

Organizations have the right to discipline, demote and fire. You may have a legitimate reason to challenge these decisions, but they do not necessarily constitute bullying. Understanding what bullying is and what it is not and making distinctions between teasing and taunting, for example, will help validate whether or not bullying is occurring.

Previously, I outlined the many forms, ways and means of bullying. Bullies can be very subtle and manipulative and frequently employ a combination of these. It is, therefore, important to relate seemingly unrelated comments, events and situations to fully portray what is happening to the target.

3. Become outraged.

The most extreme form of bullying, genocide, went on because too few citizens became outraged enough to become witnesses, defenders, resistors or activists. When we become outraged, we are more likely to correct what we believe is wrong. Had a small percentage of people in Nazi-occupied countries, or in Bosnia, or Uganda, for example, been outraged enough over what occurred, the course of history would have been different.

4. Reach out to the target.

The first piece of advice I give to the bullied is "Don't deal with it alone." The target is in a lonely place and does not believe that anyone can or will help. Go to the target and say, "I think you are being bullied; is there anything I can do to help?" This approach will let the target know s/he is not alone, and it will confirm what they suspect. If the target is too ashamed to acknowledge that s/he is being bullied, relay your observations and, if there is a pattern of bullying, indicate that s/he is not the first target.

5. Help the target "Build a Sense of Self."

Building a strong sense of self is the prerequisite to taking control of the situation and not being controlled by it.

You are in a unique position to help. Assuming you know the target, you can highlight the positive attributes s/he has. You can also contrast the positives with what you observe as negative reactions to being bullied and help the victim assess his or her sense of self.

6. Help the target become assertive.

The first step is point five: helping the target build a sense of self. The next steps are to help him or her follow points four through nine in "Advice to the Bullied."

- "Validate whether you are being bullied."
- "Understand what is motivating the bully.
- "Keep a detailed diary of what you are going through."
- "Don't fall into the bully's trap."
- "Avoid getting set up."
- "Make a formal request to have the bullying stop."

These usually fall outside of people's comfort zones. Help, coach, support and provide constructive criticism to help the target.

7. Help the target avoid causing harm.

If you feel that the target needs professional help, encourage him or her to seek it. You may have to go to the target's family or other friends for a proper intervention.

If you feel that the target has the potential of harming himself or others, you must report the situation to someone in authority. In the section "Human Resources—Part of the Problem or Part of the Solution," I outline indicators to look for. These red flags are always evident, and most extreme examples of violence could have been avoided if there were early intervention. Most leaders do not view verbal or psychological abuse as violence, or connect that these types of predatory aggression give rise to physical aggression (by both the bullied and the bully). Fill the void of leadership here and make the connection.

When you report this, you are not being disloyal to the target. You are not a snitch; you are protecting the target and others who potentially could get seriously injured or killed.

8. Request that the bully stop the bullying.

If the target is not able to handle the situation and you have a sufficiently solid relationship with the bully, indicate that you know what is going on and that it would be in his best interest to stop bullying. Point out that you are on to him/her through your own observations and that the target did not complain to you.

Alternatively, if your relationship with the bully is not solid, but is solid with the bully's immediate superior, request that s/he intervene.

9. Formally register and report.

If point number eight is not feasible or has backfired, you should report the situation to someone in authority who you absolutely trust. If there is no one you trust to properly intervene and keep it confidential, protecting both you and the target, you should consider two options:

- Submit the report to either the organization's legal counsel or external auditor (with the understanding that you will not be revealed as the source of the report and the target will not be retaliated against).

or

- Send the report anonymously to the organization's lawyer. If this is the route you take, the report should identify the bully and outline as much as you can without identifying you as the source or the target. Also, you should outline your expectation that the matter will be properly investigated and that the bullying stops. If the bullying continues and/or you and the target are subject to retaliation, file a report with the Chair of the Board of Directors, pointing out that the report was sent to the company's lawyer and what happened as a result.

10. Hold the organization and its leaders accountable.

When you report, you must be very clear about your motivation, which is to stop the bullying. Without sounding like a blackmailer, indicate that if the situation is not properly investigated and the bullying does not stop, or you and the target experience retaliation, you will take the matter further. (You don't have to say what "further" is.)

11. Help start the revolution for change.

As the bystander, you are in a powerful position to change the culture. While I caution against anger, I encourage indignation against what the targets and others in the organization are going through.

12. Build on your "Sense of Self."

Recognize that your choice to become a witness, defender, and activist has significantly strengthened your "Sense of Self"—Congratulations!

The philosopher and Holocaust survivor Emmanuel Levinas dedicated his life to understanding ethical relations between human beings. He felt that our responsibility to one another is the foundation of human community and that the basis of a meaningful life is our ability to give what we can to each other. His lessons offer parallels for the modern workplace. Bystanders who witness the abuse of others need to become defenders, resistors and activists against harsh treatment.

Redemption—Advice to the Bully

"You've got to be brave and you've got to be bold.
Brave enough to take your chance on your own
discrimination, what's right and what's wrong,
what's good and what's bad."
−ROBERT FROST

My advice to those who bully is simply stop bullying, and change or be changed.

My research shows that the majority of bullies are what I refer to as a bully who is targeted by another bully. These people usually work in cultures that condone, encourage and expect their managers to motivate by fear and intimidation and have CEOs who are also CBOs (Chief Bullying Officers). Many of these people behave outside of their value system, and all too many love to exert their power though bullying. Sadly for many, bullying is the only way they know how to get things done.

Most of the bullies I have dealt with were unhappy people who did not even like themselves and, therefore, had no problem being mean to others.

One of the purposes of the book is to "help bullies change." In the introduction, I outline the eleven things I believe need to happen for bullying to stop.

Regarding the bully, I believe:

- That an employee index be a major component on how managers are measured.

- Bullies need to be held accountable for their behaviors and actions.

- Where workplace bullying is a factor in a suicide, the organization and the bully should face criminal charges.

- Where workplace bullying causes major harm, the organization and the bully should face criminal and/or civil charges.

Another purpose of this book is to raise the level of awareness—and by raising the level of awareness, empower both the target and bystanders to force the bullying to stop and hold the organization and the bully accountable for their behaviors and actions.

While I raise the level of awareness on the risks and the costs of bullying to the individual, the family unit, the organization, and the community, I find that what really resonates with bullies is the risk they face.

For me, if the motive for a bully to stop bullying is risk avoidance, that is sufficient—not ideal—but sufficient.

I offer the following advice to the bully:

1. If you are the CBO (Chief Bullying Officer), really study this book.

Unless you change or are changed, your organization will operate in a culture of fear, you will not hear what you need to hear, your organization will not reach its full potential, the best and the brightest will not stay or join and you place your organization at risk. While I believe that bullies in your organization can stop being bullies, if you are a bully, it will, obviously, be difficult for them to do so.

2. Understand what constitutes bullying and what does not.

If you are a manager, you are expected to manage, and part of managing is to correct deficiencies and attitudes. As there are ways and means of bullying, there are ways and means of positively motivating, managing, leading and correcting deficiencies and attitudes. While this is beyond the scope of this book, there is ample work done on this and, through your employer or on your own, you should educate yourself on how to get things done without bullying.

3. Know your rights and exercise them.

Being bullied is no excuse to be a bully. If bullying is the only way to either survive or get ahead in your organization, you should seriously think about making a change. Ultimately, you will get caught and have to face the consequences of your behaviors and actions, which could include facing criminal and/or civil charges.

4. Understand the devastating impact that bullying can have on the individual, the family unit, the organization and the community.

I believe that everyone can, and should, be able to relate to this as, at some point in everyone's life, they have been a target and/ or a bystander, and/or have had someone close to them be a target. By personalizing the impact of bullying, you are better able to conclude that you have to change.

5. Don't deal with it alone: seek the advice and help of others.

If you can identify someone in your organization who is a role model, who survives and thrives without being a bully, go to that person and ask his or her advice. You might also seek the help of a career coach or psychologist. Many organizations sponsor this. If they do not, it is an investment worth making.

6. Reach out to those you have bullied and apologize.

Indicate to them that you genuinely want to change and that you want them to call you on it when you cross the line.

7. Become a role model of someone who survives and thrives without being a bully.

I encourage bullies to seek redemption; the prerequisite to this is caring. If you don't care for your fellow human being, you will have great difficulty changing your behavior. Nelson Mandela, in his book *Long Walk to Freedom*, put it so well when he wrote, "No one is born hating another person because of the colour of his skin, or his background, or his religion. People must learn to hate, and if they can learn to hate, they can be taught to love, for love comes more naturally to the human heart than its opposite."

Interdependence—Advice to Families and Friends

"The fundamental law of human beings is
interdependence.
A person is a person through other persons."
—ARCHBISHOP DESMOND TUTU

When someone is being bullied, you, as a family member or close friend, will know something is wrong based on changes in behaviors, attitudes, or physical and mental health.

As I indicate in the chapter "Overcoming It—Advice to the Bullied," people react to bullying in different ways. Some just let it happen, others get angry and retaliate. Some become bullies and take out their anger on others (often their families), while others revert to extreme measures, such as seriously injuring or killing the people who they feel are responsible for their bullying and, for others, the only way out is to commit (or attempt) suicide.

Also, I indicate in the same section that, it is my belief that people who are being bullied can do something about it in a positive and safe way. Family and/or close friends are in the best position to help.

Indicators that someone you love may be in pain:

- Avoiding activities, places or feelings

- Instability or outbursts of anger

- Loss of interest in activities or life in general

- Substance abuse

- Depression

- Guilt, shame or self blame

- Mistrust

- Physical aches and pains

How to support them:

1. Help them build a strong "sense of self."

They are dwelling on the negatives. You can shift how they feel about themselves by accentuating the positives: the good qualities they have, their accomplishments, their place at home and in the community. Encourage them to exercise and eat right. They are important factors in building a strong sense of self.

2. Don't let them fall into the bully's trap.

The bully wants to wear their targets down until it affects their performance, attendance and attitude. Encourage the bullied to resist this and focus on excelling, keeping their anger in check and avoiding confrontations with the bully.

3. Don't advise them to get out.

The majority of people who are bullied quit because they believe it is the only way to stop the bullying. Leaving an organization is an option, but it should not be the first one.

4. Seek professional help.

If you believe that the bullied family member or friend could be of danger to himself or others, insist that s/he seek professional help. If s/he refuses this, you need to advise his or her employer so they are aware that there is a risk. Similarly, if you see a significant deterioration in someone's physical health, seek professional help.

The Unthinkable

The sad reality is that bullying is a too-frequent factor in suicides or attempted suicides. If this happens in your family, you should hold the bully and the organization accountable by seeking a criminal charge and/or filing a civil suit.

The other sad reality is that bullying is a factor when an employee causes serious harm, including murder. If bullying is a factor, if a family member or close friend goes to this extreme, the bully and the organization has to bear some of the responsibility, because of inaction despite the warning signs. You must be an advocate for this.

Advice on Whistleblowing

Consider how the course of history could have been so different if people in the know reported wrongdoing. Countries and organizations put themselves at huge risk if people are afraid to report wrongdoing. Sadly, this is the case in all too many organizations. There is rarely a day where wrongdoing is not exposed in the media, which damages the brand and reputation of organizations.

Advice to Organizations

Organizations must take the lead on this, first, by ensuring they do not have a culture of fear, and second, by implementing an internal reporting system. The following is recommended:

1. There should be an independent reporting mechanism utilizing an independent third party. This third party should communicate any reported wrongdoing to two different people in the organization.

2. The policy should state that information provided must be clear, truthful and made in good faith.

3. The policy should state clearly what "good faith" means. It doesn't mean that one is always right, just that one honestly thinks one is right, or that one honestly thinks

there is a valid issue that needs reviewing by someone with appropriate skills and knowledge.

4. The policy should ask for the who, what, when, where and why—who is involved; what action/non-action does the whistleblower think is wrong; where and when did the perceived wrongdoing occur; who witnessed the behavior; and why does the whistleblower think it is wrong. Supporting documentation should be requested. These details assist the investigation and will discourage false, frivolous or bad faith claims.

5. Confidentiality must be guaranteed. No attempt to discover the identity of a whistleblower should be made. However, the policy should encourage revealing the whistleblower's name as it makes investigation easier and more effective. If the name is given, then an assurance of non-disclosure should be provided to whatever extent possible. The policy should advise that failure to provide a name or details of the alleged wrongdoing might compromise the organization's ability to investigate.

6. A strict non-retaliation policy must be stated, adhered to and enforced. It is certainly arguable that if people "in the know" have sufficient protection against retaliation, certain situations would not have occurred.

7. All reported matters should be investigated.

8. Updating the whistleblower on the investigation may be useful, while being clear that confidentiality may restrict disclosing details of the investigation to the whistleblower. The point is to assure the whistleblower that the reported wrongdoing is being investigated; otherwise,

the whistleblower may take their concerns to the media or a third party.

9. Reviewers should assume that the report was made in good faith, unless there is clear evidence rebutting that assumption. Note that this does not mean that the report is true, which must be determined based on the investigation.

10. Make it part of your organization's culture that wrong-doing will not be condoned and that everyone has a duty to report any suspected wrongdoing to a supervisor or to the organization's independent whistleblower pro-gram. This process helps ensure that the whistleblower program is publicized. One company was proud that there were no reports under its whistleblower program, only to learn that most employees were unaware of it.

11. Senior management's support for the reporting and correction of wrongdoing has to be stated clearly and unequivocally and seen to be real in both word and deed.

Furthermore, as I've said many times, the culture comes from the top and focusing on short-term gain is—too often—an indirect cause of a culture gone wrong. Former Enron CEO Andrew Fastow is now speaking out to the business community about the perils of pursuing short-term profits. He offers four lessons to avoid this trap:

1. "Is this legal?" is the wrong question. Boards too often fret about whether their actions are lawful rather than whether they're ethical. When stretching an interpreta-tion of the law as a basis for decision-making, inevitably, someone will step over the line.

2. Imagine your grandchildren will inherit the company. Mr. Fastow proposes a simple test for evaluating corporate decisions: Would you do it if the company was private and your grandkids were going to inherit it? He posits that, had the test been applied at Enron, "99 percent" of the shady practices wouldn't have been approved.

3. Have an antagonistic board member or advisor. When groupthink rules the day, board members and senior management are unlikely to speak out if they aren't comfortable with a proposed plan. Assigning a board member to the role of challenging all ideas can encourage other members to speak their mind—or, at least, consider, alternative plans.

4. Skepticism is a virtue. A culture of skepticism throughout the company should be encouraged. Employees should always feel empowered—obligated, even—to ask tough questions about the ethics and long-term value of all corporate actions."

Advice to Employees

If your employer's internal reporting system is similar to this recommendation, and you are comfortable that the system has integrity, follow this protocol. If you do not feel that confidentiality will be protected and/or there is potential for retaliation, I would advise making a report to the organization's external auditor. When you do this, seek written assurance that confidentiality is protected.

Regardless of how you report, do it in good faith, with clarity, using the facts you have or what you have heard. Don't embellish, assess, or be judgmental. You are simply reporting what you believe is wrong. Whenever I assess reports of wrongdoing, I first determine if the person is registering something they dislike vs. something they truly believe is wrong. Finally, if you observe or hear of wrongdoing, don't become the investigator. The investigation must be the responsibility of the organization. If you conduct it on your own, you could be considered a witch hunter.

Be aware too of state laws regarding whistleblowing. Eight states have specific laws preventing whistleblowers from taping wrongdoing in slaughterhouses and nursing homes, for example. The most stringent was enacted in North Carolina in January 2016. The *New York Times* reported that:

"Anyone who violates the law—say, by secretly taping abuses of elderly patients or farm animals and then sharing the recording with the media or an advocacy group—can be sued by business owners for bad publicity and be required to pay a fine of $5,000 for each day that person is gathering information or recording without authorization."

The troubling truth is that, too often, established structures in society are better equipped to silence criticism than whistleblowers are equipped to expose wrongdoing. This is evocative of a huge problem, both in the agriculture industry and the business world at large. As long as law takes the side of corporate interests over whistleblowers, industries will never improve, bad business practices will continue to go unacknowledged and most of us will be ignorant about these business practices that affect our family, friends and the food we eat.

A happy ending—John's story

John is the CEO of a large manufacturing company established by his grandparents in 1927. The company is privately held and the family owns the controlling shares. There are six manufacturing facilities, all of which are non-union, which is a source of great pride to John and his family. The company has enjoyed good relations with their employees.

In 2002, John was able to attract Ryan to run the Ajax Plant, their second largest facility. Ryan came with the right pedigree, having spent the bulk of his career in Operations with a global packaged goods company. During the extensive interview process, Ryan said all of the right things and impressed the selection committee. Ryan was the first outsider in the company's history to be brought in at this level.

John allowed each facility to operate with autonomy, within certain operating parameters and quality standards, as he believed that entrepreneurship was key to achieving superior results.

By all metrics, Ryan did a great job. Revenue, profitability, quality and service levels all exceeded plan on a consistent basis.

A number of years prior, John introduced a balanced scorecard for the business, and all departments and facilities were measured on the financials, an employee index, and a customer index. Every year, an employee attitude survey was conducted. Ryan's facility always scored well, although the participation rate averaged 70 percent: not as high as the other departments and facilities.

In 2006, the company received notice that the Ajax Plant was the target of a union organizing drive.

Given the results of the employee engagement survey conducted only six months previous, this came as a complete surprise. John's initial reaction was to trust Mary, the company's vice president of Human Resources, and Ryan, and their advice to do everything possible to keep the union out. John believed that a union could make the plant non-competitive with rising salaries, limited productivity and restrictive work practices. Mary was responsible for developing the plan to keep the union out. She immediately retained a law firm who had a reputation for avoiding unions. Ryan was responsible for all of the activities that were not handled by the labor lawyers.

The plan that Mary developed included all of the usual legal tactics as well as a number that definitely crossed the line. People who were thought to be ringleaders of the union drive had their phones monitored; some were even put under surveillance. A senior union person was even offered a bribe. Managers and supervisors were coached on how to subtly reveal the consequences if employees signed union cards or voted to certify.

John publicly suggested that the union would make the facility uncompetitive and they would have to relocate. A capacity study was done and John and others made it known that there was ample capacity in their other facilities to move production. A number of employees were fired with trumped-up allegations of wrongdoing that John was unaware of. New hires were planted to keep Ryan informed of who was doing what; many were paid under the table. Employees were pitted against employees, and emotions ran high. The legal and surveillance bills went into the hundreds of thousands of dollars.

Throughout this, Ryan was in his element; every time he spoke to John he said, "We are going to win, those bastards don't know who they are dealing with."

John kept his Board of Directors apprised of the situation, one of whom asked John, "Why do the employees feel they need a third party to represent them?" John admitted he was perplexed by it. Employees there and at the other facilities had a pay rate and benefits that were slightly ahead of competitors who were unionized and "we treat them well and with respect. This is something that we measure every year in our employee attitude survey." The Board member then asked John whether he had observed any indicators of discontent during his visit to the facility prior to the union drive. John had to answer "No," which was technically an honest answer, but he failed to mention that he had not visited the facility in two years, and, when he did, he did not go beyond the office.

The questions made John realize though that he was not close enough to the operations. All he looked at were the results, but not how they were achieved. There were a couple of managers John knew who had recently resigned from the Ajax plant and he asked for a meeting.

What they told John confirmed his worst fears. From the time Ryan took over the facility, it was run like a dictatorship. Ryan bullied the managers who, in turn, bullied the supervisors, who bullied the rank-and-file. Performance was achieved through harassment, threats and fear. Specific examples appalled John. When asked why they didn't come to him, John was told, "Ryan would ruin us if he ever found out, and everyone who works there shares this concern." John cited the employee engagement survey results. The former managers said employees didn't trust it and knew, if the results came back negative, Ryan would go on a witch hunt.

The former managers recommended that John review the turnover rate, absentee records, number of people who have been on stress leave, and the fact that very few employees, including them, did an exit interview. They also suggested that John check out Ryan's vendor contracts. "You may find they are related to Ryan's wife," one of them said.

After this meeting, John asked Mary to investigate and she reported that the turnover at the plant averaged 12 percent for production and distribution employees, and an astounding 30 percent for managers and supervisors. The absentee rate was significantly higher at Ajax than at the other facilities. Applications for stress leaves were high but, in most cases, challenged by the insurance provider at the request of the plant Human Resource manager. Mary also reported that accidents were covered up and employees stayed on salary to protect their experience ratings. Mary said she had heard rumors about the suppliers, but she didn't follow up because she was afraid of Ryan as well.

Mary further admitted that she was aware of problems, but had no idea that it was so bad. She defended her behavior saying that the engagement surveys didn't validate what she was hearing.

This was a rude awakening for John. He was frustrated with himself, betrayed, and seriously questioned whether he was now equipped to fix everything that was wrong. He also wondered, if he was so out of the loop regarding the Ajax plant, how different would he find the situation at the other facilities.

John laid out the situation to the Board with a plan. First, however, he volunteered to resign if they lost confidence in him and said, if they did, he would understand. The Board gave John a vote of confidence with the qualifier that he needed to take a more hands-on approach in running the company. The Board also unanimously agreed with John's plan.

The first step was to deal with Ryan. When John confronted him, Ryan vehemently defended what he referred to as his "aggressive management style," citing the consistent results he had delivered. He conceded that his brother-in-law owned the outside contractors and he had not declared a conflict of interest. John asked for, and received, his resignation.

John then met with the union and updated them on the actions he'd taken to avoid the Ajax plant from becoming certified and agreed to have an employee vote on whether they wanted representation. Further, he offered to meet with employees to tell them if they elected to be represented, the company would respect their decision. He also said he would retract the threats to close the plant and declare that the plant was a solid performer and could continue to be if it were unionized.

Two weeks later, the employees voted in favor of representation by a large margin. As the wages and benefits were already a bit ahead of the unionized competitors, the company and the union agreed to an incentive program that rewarded productivity, quality and service-level targets.

Concurrently, a consulting firm was hired to do a thorough cultural assessment of the organization and report back with recommendations. The company's primary objective was to gain the trust of the employees at all of their facilities. John followed all of the recommendations with one exception, which was to continue to do an engagement survey. His rationale was they had done this over the years and it failed, because, if employees do not trust leadership, they will not trust any mechanism to gauge attitudes. "From now on we are going to hear directly from our employees because they will not be afraid to express their feelings, concerns or ideas," he declared.

Not only did the company survive the economic downturn, it prospered. The Ajax plant became the number one performer and all of the other facilities exceeded their targets. The company grew, adding staff. Turnover, absenteeism, and accidents all decreased dramatically. Employees at all facilities enjoyed compensation that well exceeded the market because of the new incentive program, which was also implemented at the other facilities. The company enjoyed a great relationship with the union and, as John indicated to the union president, they were "not at all concerned about our other plants being unionized because we are going to make sure they never feel they need a third party to represent them."

Attitude or engagement surveys are no longer conducted. Instead, quarterly town hall meetings are held with all shifts in all facilities. John attends each and every one, communicates results and plans going forward, and opens the meetings for questions and comments. Today, based on the honest exchanges that take place, there does not appear to be a lack of trust.

Investor's Business Daily spent years analyzing leaders and successful people in all walks of life and they identified ten traits. John's story is an excellent example of their tenth point, which is: "Be Honest and Dependable; Take Responsibility." The key is how well you work with your organization to regain trust. The tips they give are: "bite the bullet, take control, make it right, avoid pitfalls, look through another lens, encourage honesty, solve problems faster, set the standard and move on." John, using his value system and his intuition as a leader, followed all of these tips, and then some.

Employee Activists—
Forcing a Cultural Transformation

"It is possible for a single individual to defy the whole might of an unjust empire to save his honour, his religion, his soul, and lay the foundation for that empire's fall or its regeneration."
—MAHATMA GANDHI

The closing case study, "A Happy Ending—John's Story," outlines how a positive cultural change was forced because of a union-organizing drive. This is a rare exception, as organizing drives are vigorously fought by most employers and usually make an already bad situation worse.

As I argue in this book, preventing bullying requires an organizational transformation. I hope leaders will see the benefit and logic of my argument and initiate the change. Given the entrenched attitudes that exist, I would not bank on it.

However, when leadership really starts at the top, maybe there is hope. Prince William launched an anti-bullying crusade in the summer of 2016. For those in the U.K., this is—truly—starting at the top. The magnitude of the issue of bullying is revealed in both the Pope and Prince William choosing to make it a preeminent concern. As I suggested earlier, the Pope's initiatives are grounded in conversation more than action, so far.

Prince William, however, has enlisted the support of corporate and cultural leaders in his campaign. Grounded in school bullying, the program also addresses bullying in the home and the workplace. The "Stand Up to Bullying" campaign focuses on bystanders and asks everyone exposed to bullying to stand up in defense of victims. This is truly a grassroots effort initiated at the top.

The powerful words that open this chapter are a clarion call to all who work in toxic cultures. Just as shareholder activists can force a shift in strategy, the composition of the Board, or a change in leadership, so can employees force a change in culture as key stakeholders.

The International Federation of Accountants at the United Nations Conference on Trade Development in 2010 identified "positioning risk management as a key board responsibility" and concluded "Governance is more than having the right structures, regulation and principles in place—it is about ensuring that the right behaviors and processes are in place."

Employees are in the best position to ensure the Board is made aware of the risk.

A first step is engaging others in the organization who share your concern and who you absolutely trust. Ideally, this group is representative of a cross-section of the organization.

The following is an example that illustrates how your concerns could be framed.

STATEMENT OF CLAIM

1. We are a group of [X] employees, representing a cross section of the company, who are concerned that the toxic culture that exists poses a risk to the organization and all of its stakeholders.

2. We are bringing our concerns forward so that you can ensure that the right behaviors and processes are in place.

3. Our intention and expectation is that the bullying stop.

4. The following outlines recent examples of bullying: [list the examples and provide documentation, e.g., emails comments on a blog or other social media, video, or sound recordings]

5. We recommend the following:

   • an investigation of the examples we have provided;

   • a cultural audit [here you can provide a copy of "Conducting a Workplace Assessment–Determining an At-Risk Position"];

   • appropriate action to ensure the bullying stops.

6. We have brought this matter to your attention in good faith and assume no attempt will be made to identify the source of this action, i.e., a "Witch Hunt," and no retaliatory action will be taken.

7. If, in conducting the investigation, you have questions, they may be forwarded to [I recommend obtaining a safe P.O. Box that is difficult to trace].

The statement should be sent to either the head of Human Resources or the organization's lawyer by registered post with a copy to the Chair of Audit of the Board.

If, after sixty days, there is no change in behaviors, a follow-up should be sent indicating that the situation has not changed (or has gotten worse). In this, you should request a response to the P.O. Box, outlining the organization's position on the matter.

If, after thirty days, no response is provided, you should send a letter indicating that you will be exposing the situation to major shareholders or the media.

If you or others suspect a witch-hunt or retaliation, seek immediate legal advice.

//

In conclusion, the following is the commencement address that I gave to graduates of a College of Applied Arts and Technology in Ontario, Canada, in June of 2011.

By many standards, I have lived a charmed and successful life. Like everyone, there have been setbacks, challenges and personal tragedies, all of which helped define who I am and what I stand for.

Six years ago, being diagnosed with leukemia and given a life sentence was one of those challenges.

Were it not for a miracle drug, which turned what was a fatal condition to a chronic one, I would be dead today. This experience forced me to reflect on my reason for being, and discovering that, notwithstanding the successes enjoyed, there was a void, which was, really, having made a difference. What was missing was a lack of purpose.

Today, my life is full of purpose, reflected in part through my philanthropy but, to a greater extent, it is putting a stop to what I believe to be an epidemic—bullying in the workplace.

There is no need for me to explain to you what bullying is and the devastating impact it has, other than to say bullying in schools shares many characteristics with bullying in the work place. As there are similarities, there are also differences. The most significant is that the tactics are subtler and there are fewer avenues for people to exit from the situation.

Bullies are masters of deflection, usually they discredit their targets until the targets become the villains. They "kiss up and kick down." Because they are viewed as high performers, they are treated like heroes who garner more credibility than the target.

In analyzing the demise of companies such as Enron, AIG, and Lehman Brothers, a common characteristic was that their CEOs were also CBOs—Chief Bullying Officers.

The global financial meltdown could have been avoided had people in the know reported wrongdoings. They did not, largely for fear of being retaliated against. In most cases, whistleblowers are viewed as traitors and subject to bullying as punishment for their treason.

Bullying has always occurred, however, it shames me to say that, largely because of greed, my generation has systematically created dictatorial leadership, where fear substitutes for motivation and positive leadership.

We have allowed tyranny and domination to dictate the culture in which we work.

This is the sad legacy that my generation leaves you.

For us it cannot be a question of "Can it be stopped?" It must be an assertion: "It must be stopped." For it to be eliminated, everyone has a role to play.

Every one graduating today will, at some point, become a bully, and/or be bullied and/or be a bystander.

If history is any indicator, only a small percent of you will become defenders of those who are bullied.

Where there has been genocide, which is the most extreme form of bullying, only a small percent of the population became witnesses and defenders of those who were targeted. Had the small percent been a mere 10 percent, the course of history would have had a different outcome.

The revolutions in the Middle East, with the overthrow of tyranny, is proof positive that the course of history can be changed, and serves as an inspiration to have the small percent become 10 percent.

Over your career, you will be faced with choices. The most difficult ones for you will be whether or not to be a witness and defender of those who are targeted, becoming part of the 10 percent.

This choice involves risk and requires courage. The risks of being a witness and defender are obvious. However, in making the risk assessment, consider the risk of not being that witness and defender.

Consider never having to say,

- I could have prevented the ruin of my coworker's career.

Consider never having to say,

- I could have prevented the break up of a family unit.

Consider never having to say,

- I could have helped avoid the demise of an organization.

Consider never having to say,

- I could have prevented a suicide or attempted suicide.

Consider never having to say,

- I could have prevented someone going postal and killing others.

Mahatma Gandhi put it so well when he declared, "It is possible for a single individual to defy the whole might of an unjust empire to save his honour, his religion, his soul, and lay the foundation for that empire's fall or its regeneration."

While this choice involves risk, it also yields rewards, the greatest of which is strengthening your sense of self, helping to make right what is wrong and making the lives of others free and safe from the ravages of tyranny.

By becoming part of that 10 percent, you can change the course of history.

AUTHOR'S NOTE—Organizational transformation will be the focus of my next book. My hope is to tell the stories of where there have been successful transformations, the resulting effects and how the change occurred. To help me on this, I encourage those who have experienced this kind of positive change to send me your story at info@andrewfaas.com.

Introduction

Sheryl and Don Grimme, Violence in the Workplace –
The Realities and the Options, Business Know-How.
http://www.businessknowhow.com/manage/violwork.htm

Laura Petrecca, "Bullying by the Boss Is Common but Hard to
Fix," *USA Today*, December 28, 2010.

Joel Goh, Jeffrey Pfeffer and Stefanos A. Zenios, "The Relationship
Between Workplace Stressors and Mortality and Health Costs
in the United States," *Management Science*, Volume 62, Issue 2,
March 13, 2015.

Part One

Nicole Winfield, "Pope Blasts Vatican Administration, Lists Its Sins
in Christmas Greeting," The Associated Press, December 22, 2014.
http://www.theglobeandmail.com/news/world/pope-blasts
-vatican-administration-lists-its-sins-in-christmas-greeting/
article22176415/

Jim Bronskill and Joan Bryden, "Ex-integrity Office Staffers Bristle
at Ouimet's 'Cadillac Package'," Canadian Press, March 09, 2011.
http://ipolitics.ca/2011/03/09/ex-integrity-office-staffers
-bristle-at-ouimets-cadillac-package/

Nick Davies, "Sean Hoare Knew How Destructive the News of
the World Could Be," *The Guardian*, July 18, 2011.
https://www.theguardian.com/media/2011/jul/18/sean-hoare
-news-of-the-world

Alan Greenberg and Mark Singer, *The Rise and Fall of Bear Stearns* (Simon & Schuster, 2010).

Robert Rice, *The Business of Crime* (Farrar, Straus and Cudahy, 1956).

Dana Ford, "Don Blankenship, ex-Massey Energy CEO, Sentenced to a Year in Prison," April 6, 2016. http://www.cnn.com/2016/04/06/us/former-massey-energy-ceo-don-blankenship-sentenced/

Diana Baumrind, "Effects of Authoritative Parental Control on Child Behavior," *Child Development*, 1966.

Alaa al Aswany, *On the State of Egypt: A Novelist's Provocative Reflections* (American University in Cairo Press, 2011).

Leon Festinger, *A Theory of Cognitive Dissonance* (Stanford University Press, 1962).

American Psychiatric Association, Diagnostic and Statistical Manual of Mental Disorders-IV, (American Psychiatric Association, 4th ed., 1994).

American Psychiatric Association, Diagnostic and Statistical Manual of Mental Disorders-V, (American Psychiatric Association, 5th ed., 2013).

Philip Zimbardo. www.zimbardo.com

Stanley Milgram, "The Perils of Obedience," *Harper's Magazine*, December 1973. http://harpers.org/archive/1973/12/the-perils-of-obedience/

Hon. Shawn Murphy, "Restoring the Honor of the RCMP." Addressing Problems in the Administration of the RCMP's Pension and Insurance Plans, December 2007, 39th Parliament, 2nd session, 11 and 117. http://publications.gc.ca/collections/collection_2008/parl/XC16-392-1-1-01E.pdf

Douglas Quan, "Canadian Police Officers Overworked, Understaffed, Stressed-out: Survey," Postmedia News, April 24, 2012.

Sarah Scott, "You *#%&!: Is this the end of the Toxic Boss?" *Maclean's*, September 3, 2007.

Paul Palango, *Dispersing the Fog: Inside the Secret World of Ottawa and the RCMP*, (Key Porter Books: Toronto, 2008).

Laura Payton and Alison Crawford, "7 Issues Facing the RCMP Commissioner" CBC News, October 27, 2011. http://www.cbc.ca /news/politics/7-issues-facing-the-rcmp-commissioner-1.1018704

Janet Merlo, *No One to Tell*, (Breakwater Books Ltd., 2013).

Sheila Fraser, "The Public Sector Integrity Commissioner of Canada – Report of the Auditor-General's," Office of the Auditor General of Canada December 14, 2010. http://www.oag-bvg.gc.ca

Paul Palango, *Dispersing the Fog: Inside the Secret World of Ottawa and the RCMP*, (Key Porter Books, 2008), 255.

Dr. Eli Sopow and Dr. Jeff Morley, Sourcebook RCMP Values-Driven Leadership, January 2009. http://s3.documentcloud.org /documents/4947/rcmp-sopow-reports.pdf

Tonda MacCharles, "Revolt in Senior Ranks Spurs Probe of RCMP Chief." *The Star*, July 27, 2010. https://www.thestar.com/news/ canada/2010/07/27/revolt_in_senior_ranks_spurs_probe_of _rcmp_chief.html

John Thavis, *The Vatican Diaries: A Behind-the-Scenes Look at the Power, Personalities and Politics at the Heart of the Catholic Church*, (Penguin Books, 2014).

Robert Mickens. www.globalpulsemagazine.com

Christopher Alessi, "ThyssenKrupp's Painful Revamp Pays Off," *The Wall Street Journal*, November 17, 2015.

"World's Most Admired Companies," *Fortune* magazine, March 28, 2016.

Jodi Kantor and David Streitfeld, "Inside Amazon: Wrestling Big Ideas in a Bruising Workplace," *The New York Times*, August 15, 2015.

Shana Lynch, referencing Jeffrey Pfeffer, Stefanos A. Zenios and Joel Goh, "Why Your Workplace Might Be Killing You," Graduate School of Stanford Business Insights, February 23, 2015.

Vindu Goel, "Yahoo's Brain Drain Shows a Loss of Faith Inside the Company," *The New York Times*, January 10, 2016.

Ann Tenbrunsel, Jordan Thomas, *The Street, The Bull and The Crisis: A Survey of the US & UK Financial Services Industry*, University of Notre Dame and Labaton Sucharow LLP.

Ted Sherman and Kelly Heyboer, "Rutgers Coach Mike Rice's Recent Firing Casts Spotlight on Tangled Tale," *The Star-Ledger*, April 4, 2013.

Rebecca R. Ruiz, "Report is Expected to Detail Corruption in World Track and Field," *The New York Times*, January 12, 2016.

David Zweig and John Gillespie, "Money for Nothing: How CEOs and Boards Are Bankrupting America," *Free Press*, January 4, 2011.

Ram Charan, *Owning Up: The 14 Questions Every Board Member Needs to Ask*, (Jossey-Bass, 2009).

Ram Charan, *Boards That Deliver: Advancing Corporate Governance from Compliance to Competitive Advantage*, (Jossey-Bass, 2005).

Lawrence G. McDonald, *A Colossal Failure of Common Sense: The Inside Story of the Collapse of Lehman Brothers*, (Random House Inc., 2010).

Michael Lewis, "The Man Who Crashed the World," *Vanity Fair*, August 2009. http://www.vanityfair.com/news/2009/08/aig200908

Jim Dwyer, "Integrity Takes a Toll at the Port Authority," *The New York Times*, December 17, 2015.

Andrew Faas, "Bullying: One of the Greatest Risks to the Organization," *Directors and Boards*, 2016 First Quarter.

Scott Pelley, "USADA head: I Got Death Threats During Armstrong Probe," 60 Minutes Sports, January 8, 2013. http://www.cbsnews.com/news/usada-head-i-got-death-threats-during-armstrong-probe/

Part Two

Frederic Ozanam, Lecture on Commercial Law, 1840.

The "Dignity at Work" Campaign. http://dignityatwork.org

David Beale and Helge Hoel, "Workplace Bullying, Industrial Relations and the Challenge for Management in Britain and Sweden." *European Journal of Industrial Relations* 16(2), 101–118. http://ejd.sagepub.com/content/16/2/101.short

William Hazlitt, *Characteristics, Selected Essays*, edited by Geoffrey Keynes (London: Nonsuch Press, 1930).

William Hazlitt, *The Best of Hazlitt* (London: Methuen, 1947) edited by P. P. Howe.

William Hazlitt, *William Hazlitt, Selected Writings* (Oxford University Press, 1991), edited and with introduction by Jon Cook.

Meghan Casserly, "When Snitches Get Stitches: Physical Violence as Workplace Retaliation on the Rise," *Forbes*, September 11, 2012.

National Crime Prevention Council, "What is Cyberbullying?" http://www.ncpc.org/topics/cyberbullying/what-is-cyberbullying

Robert Sutton, *Good Boss, Bad Boss: How to Be the Best . . . and Learn from the Worst*, (New York: Business Plus, 2012).

Jack Ewing, "A Top Banker's Image, Clouded," *The New York Times*, August 30, 2013.

Heinz Leymann, "The Content and Development of Mobbing at Work," *European Journal of Work & Organizational Psychology*, January 14, 2008.

Matt Taibbi, "How Wall Street Is Using the Bailout to Stage a Revolution," *Rolling Stone*, April 02, 2009.

Seth J. Prins, Lisa M. Bates, Katherine M. Keyes, Carles Muntaner, "Anxious? Depressed? You Might Be Suffering from Contradictory Class Locations and the Prevalence of Depression and Anxiety in the USA," *Sociology of Health & Illness*, August 3, 2015. http://onlinelibrary.wiley.com/doi/10.1111/1467-9566.12315/full

Leah Eichler, "The 80-hour Workweek Doesn't Work," *The Globe and Mail*, November 15, 2015.

Richard Peter and Johannes Siegrist, "Chronic Work Stress, Sickness Absence, and Hypertension in Middle Managers, General or Specific Sociological Explanations?" *Social Science & Medicine*, Volume 45, Issue 7, October, 1997.

Ellen Cobb, "Workplace Bullying: a Global Overview," *Management Issues*, July 8, 2011. http://www.management-issues.com/opinion/6235/workplace-bullying-a-global-overview/

Mark Ames, "Why Jim Badasci 'Went Postal': How Bullying Bosses and Economic Devastation Are Behind America's Latest Workplace Shooting." www.exiledonline.com

John-Paul Ford Rojas, "Bullying 'Seen as Acceptable in Army' as Survey Reveals Every Woman Questioned Was Victim of Unwanted Attention," *The Telegraph*, November 29, 2012.

Department of Defense Annual Report on Sexual Assault in the Military, Fiscal Year 2012. http://www.sapr.mil/public/docs /reports/FY12_DoD_SAPRO_Annual_Report_on_Sexual _Assault-volume_one.pdf

Shauna Lewis and Robin Perelle, "Why Most Gay Athletes Are Reluctant to Come Out," *Daily Xtra*, February 10, 2010.

Leslie Kwoh, "A Silence Hangs Over Gay CEOs," *The Wall Street Journal*, July 25, 2012.

Robbie Rogers, The Next Chapter. www.robbiehrogers.com, February 23, 2013.

"Is it Safe to Be Out in the Entertainment Industry?" Actors Equity, January 26, 2012. https://www.equity.org.uk/news-and-events /equity-news/is-it-safe-to-be-out-in-the-entertainment-industry/

Retaliation Remains Most Frequent Allegation Among Federal-Sector Discrimination Complaints, EEOC, July 6, 2011. https://www.eeoc.gov/eeoc/newsroom/release/7-6-11.cfm

Dr. Nancy Wayne, "The Bully Pulpit: Bullies in the Workplace and How to Protect Yourself." https://nancylwayne.wordpress.com /2016/07/01/the-bully-pulpit-bullies-in-the-workplace-and-how -to-protect-yourself/

Tim Field, BullyOnline. http://bullyonline.org/old/related /whistle.htm

Naomi Shavin, "What Workplace Bullying Looks Like in 2014 – and How to Intervene," *Forbes*, June 25, 2014.

Afua Hirsch, "Workplace Racism Is on the Rise – We Need Action, not Lip Service," *The Guardian*, November 10, 2015.

Race at Work Report 2015, Business in the Community. http://race.bitc.org.uk/all-resources/research-articles/race -work-report

David Maxfield, "Crucial Conversations, Influencer Training," Vital Smarts. http://www.vitalsmarts.com/

Kaj Bjorkqvist, Karin Osterman, and Monika Hjelt-Back, "Aggression Among University Employees," *Aggressive Behavior*, (1994): Volume 20, 173–184.

Joanne Royce, Bullying in the workplace blog series, Royce & Associates, November 2012.

Loraleigh Keashly, "Bullying in the Workplace: Causes, Consequences and Actions." Slides from the University of Michigan Investing in Ability 2015 series of events.

Christine Porath and Christine Pearson, "How Toxic Colleagues Corrode Performance," *Harvard Business Review*, April 2009.

Christine Porath and Christine Pearson, "The Cost Of Bad Behavior: How Incivility is Damaging Your Business and What To Do About It," *Portfolio Hardcover*, July 9, 2009.

United States Department of Labor, Safety and Health Topics. https://www.osha.gov/SLTC/workplaceviolence/

Naomi Shavin, "How Common Are Workplace Murders in America?," *New Republic*, August 26, 2015.

Kim Willsher, "Orange France Investigates Second Wave of Suicides Among Staff," *The Guardian*, March 19, 2014.

Gary Namie, "What Stopped the Bullying in 2014," 2014 WBI Workplace Bullying Survey. http://www.workplacebullying.org/2014-stops/#more-15537

Heinz Leymann and Annelie Gustafsson, "Mobbing at Work and the Development of Post-Traumatic Stress Disorders," *European Journal of Work and Organizational Psychology*, January 14, 2008.

Part Three

Hare Psychopathy Checklist, Encyclopedia of Mental Disorders.
http://www.minddisorders.com

Robert Hare. http://www.hare.org

Part Four

Emmanuel Levinas. http://levinas.sdsu.edu/

Clifton Fadiman, *The American Treasury, 1455–1955*, (New York:
Harper, 1955).

Julie Blair, "New Breed of Bullies Torment Their Peers on the
Internet." *Education Week*, February 05, 2003. http://www
.edweek.org/ew/articles/2003/02/05/21cyberbully.h22.html

M.E. Kabay, "Anonymity and Pseudonymity in Cyberspace:
Deindividuation, Incivility and Lawlessness versus Freedom
and Privacy." Paper presented at the annual conference of the
European Institute for Computer Anti-virus Research (EICAR),
Munich, Germany 16–8 March 1998.

ACKNOWLEDGMENTS

I doubt that any book can be written in isolation. Those who try, shortchange themselves and, more importantly, the reader. Writers need support, encouragement, and critical input. This, I received in spades and am forever grateful.

My partner Lee Wells helped me through the periods of self-doubt (there were many) and boosted my self-confidence. Eleanor Pope, who has been my Executive Assistant for fifteen years (which says something about both of us), has kept me focused, on track, and put some semblance of order in my scattered thoughts, sentences, and paragraphs (for those who know me, not an insignificant accomplishment).

Giving an author critical input is not an easy task, particularly if there is friendship involved—you want to be honest, but you also don't want to hurt feelings. Virginia Cirocco, Catherine Faas, Jennifer Grant, Karen Gruson, Velvet and John Haney, Ryan Jackson, Keith Juriansz, Catherine Labrosse, Susan McClelland, Bobbi Reinholdt, Maureen Ryan, and Paris Vlahovic all gave me the much needed critical, direct feedback with such kindness that it fostered even better relationships.

The partnership with Meryl Moss Media Relations and their professionalism make me appreciate the value of employees whose primary objective is to exceed the expectations of customers. Today, authors have many options, including self-publishing. As a fairly new author, the experience was rewarding and Meryl Moss and her team allowed me to focus on improving and expanding on the content, while helping me identify a larger audience for this important message. In addition to

Meryl's sterling stewardship, I'd like to thank the team who helped make this dream a reality: Catherine (Katie) Hires, Deb Zipf, and Karen Kingsley. The beautiful new cover design came about because of the talented work of John Lotte and Jeffrey Michelson.

Finally, to all of the people interviewed for this book, their stories raised my level of indignation on what all too many people have to endure every day. This has increased my passion and resolve to do what I can to stop bullying from occurring in the workplace.

Special Acknowledgement

To Rollie, Casey Girl and Rollie Jr

"New Research finds that 'man's best friend' could be life savers for veterans of the wars in Iraq and Afghanistan"
–CHRIS COLIN, *SMITHSONIAN* MAGAZINE 2012

Rollie, a magnificent, grey, regal Weimaraner with the saddest green eyes, was my constant companion during the time I was bullied and while writing the first iteration of this book.

My first dog, I adopted Rollie when he was a sixteen-month-old puppy, suffering from acute separation anguish and, as a result, was the neediest dog I ever encountered. This was okay by me as he gave so much more than he needed. I soon discovered what it really meant to be needed and, as he was dependent on me, I was dependent on him.

As a first-time author, I went through periods of writer's block and self-doubt in trying to convey my message, and extreme frustration with the technology I was using (at one point, over four thousand words evaporated into cyberspace!). Rollie was there with me through it all and, although he could not say the words, his eyes said, "Don't worry, Daddy—you can do it." Much of what was written was thought through on my daily two- to three-hour walks with Rollie. He never tired of me talking (I think out loud).

Because I was bullied, for all too-long a period, I was depressed, angry and my confidence fell. Somehow, like magic, Rollie lifted all of this negative energy—just watching his butt and tail wag on our long walks, his joy when I came home, his constant need to be close, and his unwavering trust in me, gave me such happiness. There is no question he helped me survive a horrific time and, in the process, made me a better person.

On December 2, 2012, at seven years old, Rollie passed away in my arms—looking at me with those sad, trusting eyes until I gently closed them.

This edition is dedicated to Casey Girl and Rollie Jr. Rollie would be so proud of how they take care of their Daddy.

An astonishing 95 percent of those who are bullied in the workplace suffer from Post Traumatic Stress Disorder (PTSD) and I know firsthand how effective canine therapy is as a way to deal with the most difficult situations and I encourage those who are going through the traumas of life to adopt a true healer.

ANDREW FAAS is an author, philanthropist and management advisor promoting psychologically healthy, safe and fair workplaces. Before becoming a philanthropist, he led some of Canada's largest corporations for over three decades as a senior executive. He founded the Faas Foundation, which supports non-profit organizations concerned with workplace well-being and other personal health and research endeavors. Currently he is partnering with the Yale Center for Emotional Intelligence on a groundbreaking initiative, Emotion Revolution in the Workplace, which will revolutionize the way organizations operate, leveraging the power of emotional intelligence. Also he has partnered with Mental Health America (MHA) in the overall initiative to promote psychologically healthy, safe and fair workplaces.

Yale *Center for Emotional Intelligence*

Lightning Source UK Ltd.
Milton Keynes UK
UKOW01f2041130717
305296UK00011B/547/P